# BENCHMARKING

This book is dedicated to all those people who, like myself, never have the time, inclination or staying power to 'read the instructions' first. The proverbial 'bulls' who rush at every task, tackling everything head on, only stopping to ask 'Why didn't you tell me?' when something goes wrong. This book will tell you just what you need to know to make your benchmarking successful – and no more.

## FULL BENCHMARKS

1  Why Benchmark?
I'm quite in the dark
Is it some weird graffiti
Done perhaps for a lark
In the Park?

2  Not so crude!
It's for a firm's good
By comparison making
Not odious but clued
Where they stood

3  Keep abreast
Of your rivalry's best
Then advance a step further
Outstripping the rest
With keen zest.

4  So maintain
No weak links in the chain
Competitively studying
How most surely to train
And avoid a brain drain
          Just Benchmark!

Norman Harry Codling (1912–1994), 1993

Over the past decade numerous books, brochures, pamphlets and cartoons have appeared on benchmarking. The above is, however, the first and – as far as I am aware – the only poem on the subject.

# BENCHMARKING

**Sylvia Codling**

Published by
Gower Publishing Limited
Gower House
Croft Road
Aldershot
Hampshire GU11 3HR
England

Gower
Old Post Road
Brookfield
Vermont 05036
USA

British Library Cataloguing in Publication Data
Codling, Sylvia
  Benchmarking
  1. Benchmarking (Management)
  I. Title
  658.4'013

ISBN 0 566 07926 7

Library of Congress Cataloging-in-Publication Data
Codling, Sylvia.
    Benchmarking / by Sylvia Codling.
      p.   cm.
    Includes bibliographical references and index.
    ISBN 0-566-07926-7
    1. Benchmarking (Management).   2. Benchmarking (Management)—Case
  studies.   I. Title
  HD62.15.C564   1998                                                98-5372
  658.5'62–dc21                                                          CIP

Typeset in Century Schoolbook by Raven Typesetters and printed
in Great Britain by MPG Books Ltd, Bodmin

# CONTENTS

# LIST OF FIGURES

# LIST OF TABLES

# PREFACE

When *Best Practice Benchmarking; The Management Guide* was published in 1992 it was the first book in Europe to deal with the subject. There was virtually no reference material and very little data in the public domain. Those companies who were doing it were keeping very quiet about it and those who were wondering whether they ought to do it were at a loss for where to go for common sense and advice.

With gathering momentum since that time, texts covering the application of benchmarking in every aspect and virtually every industry have mushroomed. Theories and case studies abound.

The same period has also witnessed a tremendous growth in the number of 'experts', 'databases' and networks which profess to provide the answers – or confuse the public, depending who you talk to!

Yet, despite this, an increasing number of managers say to me: 'Just tell me what I need to know and let me get on with it.' If you have ever said that, this book is for you. It is intended as a quick no frills read which will bring benchmarking down to earth for you.

However, there are all sorts of tools and techniques for managers. Do you need to know about this one? What makes it so special? The answer to the first question is 'Yes'. Why? Because the answer to the second question is that benchmarking is probably the single most effective tool for improving key aspects of the business – whether your objective is transformation or continuous incremental change.

And change, to a greater or lesser degree, is inevitable; it does not have to come about as a result of benchmarking but you cannot carry out benchmarking without making a difference. Nor should you consider the technique if you are not prepared to learn from other individuals, organizations or cultures. This is because benchmarking is also about discovering – in fact, it is developing as one of the most effective ways of transferring knowledge and new ideas across and between organizations.

Developing continuous learning and managing endless change are rapidly becoming the hallmarks of 'successful' firms and this makes benchmarking all the more important since it intrinsically involves a bit of both. It encourages questions about how we compare with others on a like-for-like basis and helps us identify how their performance compares with ours and, hence, where the potential for improvement lies. It is about active measurement and comparison.

Measurement is critical, but it is only part of the story. The bulk of it is about understanding why others do things more effectively and efficiently. From this we learn and adapt what is done in order to bring about improvements which enable us to perform better. This results in incremental, significant or transformational change.

So, to go back to the original question: 'Do we need to know about benchmarking?' As the late W. Edwards Deming said 'You don't have to do these things. Survival is not essential.'[1] This book will help you judge for yourself whether benchmarking is appropriate for your organization and how best to initiate your first projects. It is divided into three parts:

Part 1, 'Before you start', provides background information and provokes consideration of supporting frameworks as well as detailing the steps of the benchmarking methodology.

Part 2, 'On your way' is about the continuing journey and making benchmarking a part of the way you do things in your organization. In the true spirit of turning theory into practice, Part 3 comprises a case study which was the winning submission in the 1997 European Best Practice Benchmarking Award™.[2] This annual event draws entries from all sectors of enterprise across the European Community. This case study provides an excellent example of one organization's experiences and learning through benchmarking a process which is applicable in every field of endeavour – vacancy filling.

The fourth and final part of the book comprises various information and references.

Sylvia Codling

## NOTES

1  Deming, W. Edwards (1982), *Out of the Crisis*, Cambridge: Massachusetts Institute of Technology.
2  Awarded annually by The Benchmarking Centre Limited based in Gerrards Cross, Buckinghamshire, UK. Full details of the award and submission criteria are available from the Centre – see Appendix 2: 'Useful contacts'.

# ACKNOWLEDGEMENTS

Very little that we achieve is ever done alone. This is arguably nowhere more true than in the case of book-writing. Personally, I owe my deepest appreciation to my husband, Brian, who, over the gestation period for this text has been, in turn, sounding board, mentor, critic, slave-driver, restorer of sanity and chef. I am indebted to him also for the many hours spent patiently reading version after version.

Books are about ideas. The best are those that are shared and built on. I wish to thank the many people who, over the years, have aired and shared their views with me and enabled the ideas presented here to develop.

Finally, I owe my professor at City University Business School, Ronnie Lessem, a special 'thank you' for suggesting many moons ago that perhaps I should write a book. Two books, and numerous articles later, I am still keen to acquire the knack!

SC

# ACKNOWLEDGEMENTS

# INTRODUCTION

Before getting started with your own benchmarking project it is worth spending a little time getting acquainted with how modern benchmarking itself has evolved.

The story begins with the Xerox Corporation in the United States during the early 1980s when they found themselves in sudden crisis. Having invented the Xerography process, the company experienced phenomenal success and growth through the 1960s and 1970s. The unique circumstance of having worldwide patents on their machines meant that by the middle of that decade they held 100 per cent of the market share. This provided them with another 'first': they reached $US1 billion in annual sales faster than any corporation in the United States had ever done before. They had no competitors worth mentioning – at least, that they were aware of!

However, even though Xerox did not realize it, the rivals were there, waiting and preparing in the wings, for the moment which they knew was coming. It came in 1978 when Xerox's patents expired and the Japanese swept into the market. They rapidly gained market share to the extent that within two years Xerox was down to just 20 per cent.

The first reactions were the familiar 'made in Japan' or 'not invented here' excuses. 'The products must be cheap and nasty.' 'The Japanese must be dumping product in the US.' 'The customers would soon learn the error of their ways.' But they did not. They bought more Japanese product. Xerox had to find out why.

What they found astounded them. The quality was far better than their own, the delivery performance was way ahead, the Japanese cared about and were consistent in servicing their customers, they were quicker at updating the products and making them better – and they were only half the price of the nearest comparable Xerox machines.

Having found out the 'why', Xerox then had to find out 'how' the

Japanese did this. They were fortunate in having a sister company based in Japan – Fuji Xerox. So Xerox got hold of a photocopier and stripped it down, and rebuilt it – a technique known today as reverse engineering. That told them part of the story: things like how many nuts, bolts and switches were used; what the differences in technology were. This kept the Xerox engineers busy for a while. Until they realized that what they had so far discovered told them a great deal about 'what' the competition was doing but very little about the 'how' it managed to do it and deliver the products at such a competitive price.

The 'what' provided the standards which the engineers had to aim for – what we now recognize as 'the benchmarks' – but it was answering the 'how' which heralded the real 'birth of benchmarking' as we know it today. Xerox started examining how it did things – its processes – and finding others whom they believed did it better: American Express, for instance, on the invoicing process. Then they compared the two ways of working and improved, adapted and changed the way they did things to incorporate the better ways of operating – or 'best practices' – which they had found. Over a period of a few years improvements in quality, delivery and service enabled them to claw back market share, notably from Japanese competitors, until in 1991 they won the prestigious Malcolm Baldrige[1] national quality award.

The full story of Xerox's early experiences with the technique we now call benchmarking is related in Bob Camp's first book.[2] The combination of this, and the example provided by the company's return from the brink, provoked other companies' curiosity about the technique. Initially, it was just a US 'fad' but gradually it began to be taken up with varying success by European-based companies, notably IBM and Rank Xerox, with US links. The first survey into the subject carried out in the UK[3] indicated a very low awareness of benchmarking, with most activity going on in financial and human resource areas. Asked about barriers to the take-up of benchmarking and the overwhelming majority of managers cited lack of knowledge, either of the concept itself or of relevant information. Reliable and comparable data about and from 'best in class' companies was the next biggest hurdle referred to. However, there was also repeated testimonial to arrogance, complacency in traditional markets and a prevalence of 'not-invented-here' attitudes. With what may have been a flash of honesty, one manager cited 'fear of comparison' as the real constraint. Surprisingly, cost and lack of managerial time – today seen as considerable hindrances – hardly featured.

By 1993, a survey[4] conducted amongst a sample of Times Top 1000 company executives showed that 32 per cent claimed to be 'doing it', although 25 per cent did not understand the technique, 26 per cent had not thought about introducing it and 17 per cent, having considered it at board level, believed it was inappropriate to their companies.

By 1996 a leading firm of consultants reported[5] that benchmarking had become the third most 'popular' management tool in organizations. Coincidentally, around this time it began to attract serious attention at government[6] and international levels with organizations such as the European Commission[7] and the Commonwealth Secretariat[8] sponsoring activities in order to raise the competitiveness, not just of individual firms but of nations.

It continues to gather advocates as, with the benefit of considerable hindsight, companies such as Rank Xerox, Texas Instruments, Shell, TNT Express, Rover, Milliken and IBM, are able to testify to the considerable savings and benefits to be gained.

The application of benchmarking has undergone a number of reincarnations over the years but the hunger for finding and learning from best practices in order to increase competitive advantage appears insatiable. At first, the focus was on stemming losses and gaining market share, in other words averting a potential crisis. However, successive deep recessions over the past ten years have resulted in many extremely lean, efficient firms with virtually no 'fat' to bolster future growth. Already extremely competitive, frequently the companies whose 'best practices' others aspire to emulate, they face the challenge of continuing to grow and increase returns to their stakeholder groups. These leaders now question how they can use benchmarking to stimulate growth instead of using it solely to become increasingly efficient.

Their experiences are leading to even more extensive use of benchmarking and will provide the route maps and templates which tomorrow's leaders will follow.

In the same way that mankind keeps striving for Olympic gold in every aspect of sporting endeavour, the race is set to continue for 'best practice' gold in corporate life.

## NOTES

1   The Malcolm Baldrige national quality award was introduced in the USA in 1987 with the objective of providing firms with an incentive to improve the quality of their products and services.
2   Now regarded as a classic, *Benchmarking: The Search for Industry Best Practices which Lead to Superior Performance* was published by ASQC Press in 1988 and tracks Xerox's introduction of the technique.
3   The search for superior performance conducted by S. Codling, 1991, among a sample of approximately 140 leading UK companies.
4   Coopers & Lybrand Survey of Benchmarking in the UK 1993, repeated 1994.
5   Bain & Co 1996.

6   The series of Competitiveness White Papers produced in the UK from 1994 to 1996 referred increasingly over the period to the importance of benchmarking.

7   Director General III Industry is responsible for supporting several major initiatives aimed at providing support at European level for benchmarking: e.g. the World Class Standards Network (WCSN), a consortium of 16 organizations drawn from universities, centres of excellence and commercial companies to develop a common best practice database; a second project aims at building a Framework for European Benchmarking in order to create greater synergies among activities and to add value to national and individual initiatives already in place.

8   The Commonwealth Secretariat was the major sponsor in 1997 of an event to 'Restructure Government for Organizational Excellence', which brought together government representatives and speakers from seven different countries at a five-day convention in South Africa.

# BEFORE YOU START

# CHAPTER 1

# WHAT IS BENCHMARKING?

Benchmarking is the most powerful technique for gaining and maintaining competitive advantage. Why? Because it drives best practice oriented continuous improvement through the organization. The perpetual goal is to achieve measurably better performance than the rivals.

Whatever it is that you decide you want or need to improve, you

○ analyse the position you are currently in
○ find someone who is performing measurably better, and
○ learn from them what they are doing to achieve that performance
○ you then adapt your practices and processes as a result of that learning and so implement relevant changes which will effect superior performance in your organization.

It is not a passive exercise. Finding out what the 'best practice' standards are and how they are achieved should always lead to positive actions being taken. These should enable you to close the gap between how you are currently performing and how much better you could be doing. The distance between these two points is established through comparison with the better performers, while closing the gap is achieved through the changes or adaptations you make to your process as a direct result of the lessons learned from the benchmark company. The ceaseless reiteration of this process enables you to develop the best practices for your organization.

Rigorous interpretations of benchmarking were rare at the beginning of the 1990s. There were, and are, many advocates of the 'You show me yours, I'll show you mine' principle. Moreover, many people readily supported a technique which involved visiting, or being visited by, reputable organizations – often in far-flung locations – to glean 'good ideas' and 'swap stories'. Renowned 'excellence' guru, Tom Peters, advocated it as 'creative swiping' and 'stealing shamelessly'.

Dubbed 'industrial tourism', this activity, though fun and attractive for the participants, rarely led to recognition, never mind implementation, of significant and sustainable improvement opportunities. One major public organization nicknamed the activity 'Springtime in Paris'. It was a regular occurrence when senior managers would travel far and wide to see what their counterparts in other countries were doing. Certainly this provides time out of the usual environment, which is stimulating and can make people receptive to different perceptions and new ideas – no bad thing. However, enthusiasm and good ideas alone do not necessarily lead to implementation of best practice. Little serious or sustained improvement is likely to result. Months later, if anyone asks what the outcome of the visit was, the most likely response is that it was a jolly interesting trip but, of course, 'the wrong people went really'.

## ■ BENCHMARKING AS A PERFORMANCE COMPARISON TOOL

It soon became apparent that real gains were more likely to arise from systematic and rigorous 'benchmarking' comparison and analysis of performance data; for instance:

○ return on investment
○ inventory turns per year
○ absenteeism rates
○ miles per gallon
○ output per employee
○ operations per surgeon per day
○ GCSE 'passes' per school per year.

The best performer was labelled 'the benchmark'[1] and comparison against this resulted in a ranking, or league table. Sometimes this was useful. Frequently, however, it led to criticism particularly when it was carried out by third parties. 'They' (collecting the data) did not understand 'our' industry, circumstances, strategy and so on. 'And, anyway,' the argument continued, 'the numbers begged more questions than they answered.' They were, in fact, just the tip of the iceberg.

## SECTOR INVOLVEMENT

In the UK, education sector representatives were among the first to feel the frustration of having their performance judged according to their ranking. How could the activities of a school in a run down urban area be compared fairly with one in an affluent suburb? Even if the teacher to child ratio was the same, virtually every other aspect was likely to be different. However, the School Effectiveness Division of the UK Department for Education and Employment published a document[2] in 1995 which 'benchmarked' the employment of school budgets. The project, on which this reported, compared expenditure under particular cost headings in different schools. It then set out ways in which schools might make best use of these comparisons to improve the effectiveness with which they used their financial resources.

While the initial data collection provided the key for the comparison, the real value of the exercise, and the reasons for the emerging differences, came from discussing the findings at the regular meetings held at each stage of the project. Teachers realized that they could improve their schools' performance not just by securing increased funding, but by learning how some of the more efficient schools were using theirs. Thus resource was freed up for deployment elsewhere. As one head teacher commented:

> For 1995/96 we have employed five classroom assistants – the benchmarking project both justified the value of this decision, and demonstrated that we could afford to do this within our staff costs budget.[3]

The medical profession also came under the audit microscope and displayed much the same anxiety. How could usage rates of a critical surgery theatre in a hospital be compared with one used for relatively minor surgery? However, once the 'anger' of the league tables was aired, hospital staff realized that they could learn from others, both in their own field and outside it. How, for example, could they increase the usage rates of the theatres, many of which had stood idle for large parts of the day?

One of the first hospitals in Europe to compare itself with another sector in order to learn how to become more efficient was the Karolinska in Sweden. As a result of comparisons with automotive manufacturing it reduced the average loss of time of 59 minutes between operations by more than half. It decreased the emphasis on certain theatres being dedicated to particular types of operation and carried out those of similar length and complexity in the same one. This enabled the closure of four of the 16 theatres, while increasing the total number of operations in the first year of the project by over 2 000 to 28 000.

The UK tourism industry also came into the limelight with a much publicized report[4] which compared bed and breakfast (B&B) establishments across the country by way of 'informing' the public at home and abroad of the differing standards they could expect to encounter.

The work was based on previous research which confirmed the criteria against which hotel customers decide on their holiday or business location. Cleanliness, comfort and convenience of the bedroom and bathroom, along with friendly and efficient service were top of the list. As the customers become increasingly demanding future success would, the report suggested, be harder to earn. Helping each other by sharing best practice was recognized as a way to raise the competitiveness of the industry.

Again, criticized at first, the report subsequently led to a number of hoteliers accepting the challenge to compare their businesses against the best. Realizing that even small inexpensive improvements can make a marked difference and boost profits is providing impetus for transforming the industry.

## ■ BENCHMARKING 'MODELS'

A number of national and international quality awards[5] have been initiated in recent years as one country after another faces the challenge of incentivizing its industrial and service base to become more competitive in the face of global competition. These provide visible, public 'excellence' goals for organizations to aim for, as well as common improvement assessment criteria against which to measure and monitor activity. They require applicants to show evidence that they have measured their performance and initiated improvements and also that they have compared their operations and practices against adjudged or perceived better performers in and outside their sector.

The assessment criteria require more than a snapshot of performance: trends, levels and comparisons need to have been tracked over a period of time – usually three years. Applicants must show whether and how they have used the comparative information to help them adapt their processes and practices in order to achieve measurable improvements in their own performance, results and customer satisfaction levels.

The models have evolved a further use to stimulate and generate competitiveness. In a number of industries, notably motor manufacturing and food, consortia groups have been brought together[6] via a facilitated process to compare their performance against the models. 'Best practices' thus identified become role models for sector-wide improvements.

## BENCHMARK DATABASES

As a result of the relentless demand for performance benchmarks and the consequent number of studies which have been conducted a number of databases have been developed. Their contents are invaluable to organizations seeking the 'tip of the iceberg' indicators. They also provide a useful, sometimes essential, picture of how organizations compare with each other on generic measures such as:

○ delivery reliability
○ scrap rates
○ component set-up times
○ absenteeism.

As such they are extremely useful for gaining a baseline. However, gathering such benchmarks is just one precursor to benchmarking itself.

## BENCHMARKING PROCESSES TO UNDERSTAND AND ADAPT BEST PRACTICES

A benchmark is a surveyor's mark, used as a reference for determining further heights and distances. In the context of corporate performance, the benchmark is a 'standard of business excellence' against which others can measure and compare their performance. It testifies that a certain level of capability is possible but does not clarify the means by which it is achieved. Measuring and comparing against a benchmark thus leads to some fundamental questions concerning conditions and circumstances.

These can be explored by focusing on processes. The efficiency and effectiveness of these may be responsible for the benchmark performance and can underpin the success (or otherwise) of an organization.

Process benchmarking is now widely recognized as the most powerful development of the technique. Furthermore, the relationship and interaction between processes, corporate strategy and culture provide a new perspective from which to develop significant and sustainable competitive advantage. However, this demands a new perspective on measurement and the determinants of success.

## NEW MEASUREMENT PERSPECTIVES

The decision about what to measure is one of the initial hurdles managers must cross when benchmarking.

The success of a business has, in the past, been largely a reflection of its financial standing. Performance measurement was a matter of comparing some or all of an organization's finances such as capital asset turnover, net return on direct assets or investment, and profit per unit of output activities. Analyses were conducted to compare present performance with the past and, based on that, targets were set for the future.

The numbers could be analysed in different ways to provide varying scenarios affording a variety of perspectives on the success or otherwise of the firm. Not only were they open to different interpretations, they were necessarily retrospective. As such they were little help in a rapidly changing environment for identifying potential failure points or sources of problems as they occurred.

As far back as the beginning of the 1990s, an article in the *Harvard Business Review*[7] signalled the revolution brewing in performance measurement. 'Within the next five years', writes the author Robert G. Eccles, 'every company will have to redesign how it measures its business performance.'

'For several years', he continues, 'senior executives in a broad range of industries have been rethinking how to measure the performance of their businesses. They have realized that new strategies and competitive realities demand new measurement systems. Now they are deeply engaged in defining and developing those systems for their companies.'

The dawning realization was that financial figures represented only one perspective among many on the emerging scorecard of measures which needed to be balanced. Market share, customer satisfaction, quality of products and of working life also required status in determining strategy, promotions, bonuses and other rewards. Senior executives were noticing that the growing trend towards customer centred strategies was being undermined by the traditional financial measurement system. This meant that when 'push came to shove' short-term financial considerations won the day. One manufacturing organization reorganized its measurements, placing earnings per share (originally at the top of the list) at last place, preceded by customer satisfaction, cash flow, manufacturing effectiveness and innovation.

A report on the role of business in a changing world[8] which was issued in 1995 emphasized this point. It stated that financial performance by itself

> does not gauge the overall health of a business. It neither defines competitive performance, nor measures the broader value created through product quality, speed of response and service. Companies which rely solely on financial measures of success are ... denying themselves the opportunity to improve returns.

Today organizations must get the facts about how they measure up and compare with others on a real-time basis across a range of success factors. Those that aspire to World Class[9] performance have an even greater imperative to improve daily. They must build into their measurement activities the means for keeping an eye on emerging technologies and innovations from other industrial and geographical sectors. All firms need to find internal efficiency improvements and external economies if they are to outstrip the competition.[10]

## ALIGNING BENCHMARKING WITH STRATEGY

Continuous improvement must be aligned with the long-term strategy and objectives of the business. No organization can afford to utilize resources without regard for its overall health and development. The focus is on the measurement of critical success factors which enable the organization to meet strategic objectives. In defining measures, management must decide what the key indicators of performance are, how they relate to one another and how they can be used to track the short, medium and long-term health of the business. For instance, having identified 'quality' as a strategic weapon, many firms have introduced defect rates, reject rates, response and delivery time as key measures.

Thus, the role of benchmarking as a tool to increase competitiveness is extensive. It not only helps firms compare themselves on their existing measures with the current 'benchmark' performers, it also enables the development of new strategic measures against which to track performance. Many of these are likely to focus on previously 'unseen' operations. In order to gauge how well the company is performing against the new internal measures, managers are required to look for external comparators. In this way they may discover opportunities for improvement that are orders of magnitude beyond what they would otherwise have thought possible. Hence, benchmarking is transforming managerial mind-sets and perspectives.

The ability to replace incremental improvement with major leaps forward is the essence of benchmarking's power.

Securing these, however, is not a matter of chance. In order to gain the full benefit, firms must adopt a rational and rigorous framework. The next chapter therefore focuses on the detailed methodology which provides this clear framework for, and route map to, successful benchmarking.

## NOTES

1   Now most usually defined as 'the highest recorded standard of excellence'.
2   DfEE (1995), *Benchmarking School Budgets: Sharing Good Practice*, DfEE Publications Centre, London.
3   Ibid., p. 5.
4   Department of Heritage (1996), *Benchmarking for Smaller Hotels*, Department of National Heritage, London.
5   The German Ludwig Erhard Award and the Icelandic and Russian Quality Award, both initiated in 1997; the European Best Practice Benchmarking Award™ initiated in 1995, awarded annually by The Benchmarking Centre Limited; the European Quality Award initiated in 1992; the UK Quality Award initiated in 1994, the latter two made annually by the European Foundation for Quality Management and the British Quality Foundation respectively.
6   The Society of Motor Manufacturers and Traders (SMMT) and Leatherhead Food Research Association.
7   Eccles, Robert G. (1991), 'The Performance Measurement Manifesto', *Harvard Business Review*, Jan/Feb.
8   (1995), *The RSA Inquiry: Tomorrow's Company*, Aldershot: Gower.
9   Simultaneous high productivity and high quality. Roberts, Peter and Thayer, Betty (1994), '*Worldwide Manufacturing Competitiveness; 2nd Lean Enterprise Report*', London: Andersen Consulting.
10  Ibid.

CHAPTER

# 2

# PLANNING YOUR BENCHMARKING ACTIVITY

One reason why benchmarking has been so readily adopted by firms is because the basic concepts and principles are easy to understand: analyse what you must do well in your business to be (more) competitive, find someone who does it better than you, learn from them how and then establish what you need to do to improve your operations.

Getting on and doing it ought to be just as simple. Which it is – as long as you follow a proven path. You should also develop a common benchmarking language, framework and methodology for your organization. This will make communication less complex as well as helping the transfer of learning and understanding across the firm.

One of the perceived problems with benchmarking is finding relevant and accessible partners. However, once the communication channels are opened there may be no need to step outside your own operations. As Texas Instruments' Chief Executive identified in 1994: 'If we only knew what we know at TI'.[1]

In other words, it is not just elsewhere that best practices are to be found. Benchmarking may open up the dialogue between different departments, sites and locations and for the first time firms recognize that they have their own excellent practices. Often, these exist in discrete pockets rather than being common across all locations where the same process is carried out. Enabling those who are not performing so well to learn from the excellent practices can generate substantial savings. In the case of Texas Instruments these amounted to more than £1.3 billion over three years.

As benchmarking has developed into a recognized technique, a common methodology has evolved. This is based on the logical order in which things need to be done to achieve results. Although there are many variations on a theme, the model shown in Figure 2.1.[2] has been adopted by many organizations. It provides a generic route map for projects and the sequence of 'plan', 'analyse', 'action', 'review' is simple to remember and repeat.

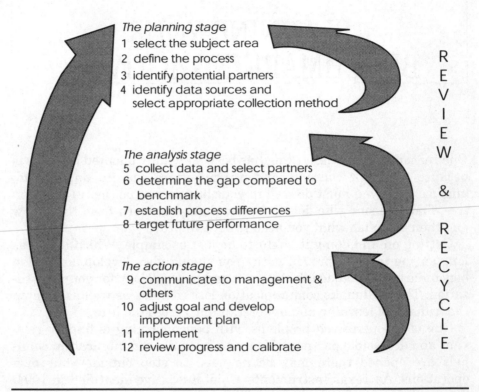

THE BENCHMARKING
PROCESS

*The planning stage*
1 select the subject area
2 define the process
3 identify potential partners
4 identify data sources and
   select appropriate collection method

*The analysis stage*
5 collect data and select partners
6 determine the gap compared to
   benchmark
7 establish process differences
8 target future performance

*The action stage*
9 communicate to management &
   others
10 adjust goal and develop
   improvement plan
11 implement
12 review progress and calibrate

R
E
V
I
E
W

&

R
E
C
Y
C
L
E

Figure 2.1    Benchmarking methodology

## BENCHMARKING METHODOLOGY: FIRST STAGE – PLANNING

### STEP 1: SELECT THE SUBJECT AREA

One of the most important considerations when benchmarking is deciding where to start (Figure 2.2). Hence, a more detailed explanation of
this crucial first planning step is included than for subsequent steps.

First, it is important to realize that you should not benchmark everything in sight. Focus your efforts where improvements will bring significant advantage to the business. There are a number of ways in
which you can identify these:

THE BENCHMARKING PROCESS

*The planning stage*

1.  select the subject area
2.  define the process
3.  identify potential partners
4.  identify data sources and select appropriate collection method

---

*Figure 2.2    First stage steps of benchmarking methodology*

O   traditional planning perspective
O   core competencies perspective
O   customer perspective
O   business objectives perspective
O   business excellence perspective.

The strengths and weaknesses of each are given below.

## Traditional planning perspective

Most firms, regardless of size, incorporate 'planning' as a key activity. In larger firms this is likely to be a separate function (such as the planning department), whereas in smaller operations it is more likely to be included within a specific 'job' (Planning Manager) or as part of a combination of roles (Finance and Planning Manager). If your organization is structured in this traditional manner, you may find that it is most logical to initiate the benchmarking debate with the corporate planning people. They will be well versed in the traditional planning questions and ensuring that benchmarking becomes a key consideration in their deliberations will be fundamental in embedding the technique within the organization (Figure 2.3).

---

WHERE TO START BENCHMARKING BASED ON THE TRADITIONAL PLANNING QUESTIONS

O   Which business are we in?
O   In which aspect of our business do we have to excel in order to gain market place advantage?
O   What would make the most significant improvement in our customer relationships?
O   Which single area, if improved, would make the most significant contribution to our bottom line results?
O   How will improvement in this area impact on other parts of the business?

---

*Figure 2.3    The traditional planning perspective of business*

*Strengths*
❐  Encourages benchmarking to be applied in a strategic context.
❐  Requires dialogue at high level thus increasing the visibility of, and level of commitment to, benchmarking.
❐  A high level 'champion' for benchmarking in the organization may emerge.

*Weaknesses*
○  Benchmarking can become just a planning activity.
○  May restrict potential for step change if previous thinking is maintained.

## Core competence perspective

Core competencies are the combination of strategic business capabilities which provide marketplace advantage (Figure 2.4). Essentially they are the unique abilities which the organization has developed over time based on its technology, experience, people, coupled with other intrinsic assets such as culture and learning ability. Hewlett Packard, for example, have identified their competence as the combination of measurement, computing and communications – or MC squared, as they call it.[3]

The basic theory is that organizations, like individuals, have a set of intrinsic assets which, if recognized and developed, can provide a competitive advantage in the marketplace. A person may, for instance, have all the inherent qualities that make an international concert pianist. These could remain dormant, could be partially developed through self-realization into a hobby, or they could be recognized early on and honed to excellence through hours of practice and performance. Organizations, likewise, have inherent qualities – ability to innovate (e.g. 3M), or to communicate (e.g. BSkyB) which may follow a similar developmental pattern.

They are assets and knowhow which have been accumulated over the period of its existence and combine:

○  the founding principles, services or product expertise
○  plus the experience accumulated by the sum of the employees over the intervening period
○  plus the skills which it has developed to exploit its niche
○  plus the learning it has assimilated from its interactions in the market place and internally.

The cumulative result is different, indeed unique, in each case.

Increasingly, organizations need to focus on, and hone, their 'uniqueness'. Prioritizing benchmarking activity in this manner will clearly

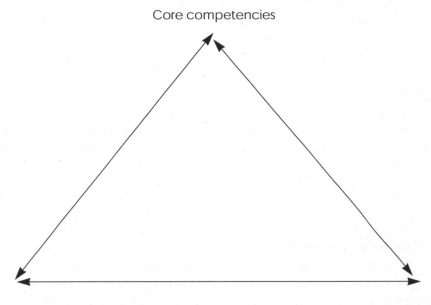

Core competencies

Key business processes                    Critical success factors

KEY
*Core competencies:* the combination of individual strategic
business capabilities which provides marketplace advantage
*Key business processes:* those processes which embody the
competencies and which influence the customer's perception of the
business
*Critical success factors:* measures of how each process performs in
terms of economy, effectiveness and efficiency

*Figure 2.4     Model showing linkages between core competencies, key business
processes and critical success factors*

contribute towards achieving competitive advantage. Furthermore, it
should be understood that there is no single 'best practice' but a
topology based on dimensions of culture and strategy.[4] Thus, it cannot
simply be imported or copied from elsewhere but needs to be moulded
to the requirements of the enterprise at the present state of its development.

*Strengths*
❏     A clear link is made between the core competencies and the busi-
      ness processes which enable them to be 'delivered' into the mar-
      ketplace.

❐   The key processes are those which influence the customer's perception of the business so this approach forces the organization to look at itself from the outside.
❐   Any resultant improvements would have a direct impact on key elements of the business.

*Weaknesses*
○   Must be done at the top of the organization or business unit where time or priorities may constrain the required discussion.
○   Can take time if competencies have not before been discussed at top level.
○   May require several iterations before competencies are fully identified.


## Customer perspective

The last decade of the twentieth century has played host to the customer revolution. Like the agricultural and industrial revolutions before it, this has shifted fundamentally the driving force of economic activity. Increasingly, businesses are framing the delivery of their goods and services in the context of meeting customer needs and expectations. Delivering customer satisfaction is now equal to providing quality goods and services as a prerequisite for doing business. Pursuing 'customer delight', if not 'customer intimacy' strategies are the trends of the future.

Hence, any firm which aspires to adopt 'best practice' must necessarily consider the viewpoint of its customers when considering where to initiate significant improvement activity through benchmarking (Figures 2.5 and 2.6).

---

DECIDING WHERE TO BENCHMARK BASED ON THE CUSTOMER'S PERCEPTION

○   Establish what makes a difference in the customers' eyes between an ordinary supplier and an excellent one
○   Set standards for those things according to the 'best' practice that can be found
○   Learn how the 'best' companies meet those standards
○   Adapt and apply lessons learned from those approaches and ideas to meet and exceed the customers' requirements
○   Ensure the best practices are shared across all parts of the company

---

*Figure 2.5    The customer perspective of the business*

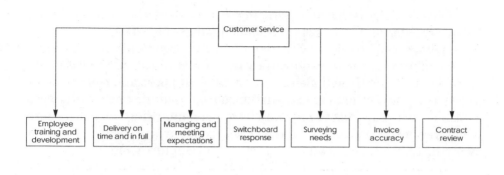

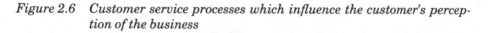

*Figure 2.6    Customer service processes which influence the customer's perception of the business*

## Strengths

☐    Establishing the customer's expectations and perspectives of best practice is essential in modern business planning.

☐    Written and verbal surveys provide effective ways of finding out what customers think of the quality of products or services which the business supplies to them.

☐    Equally they can provide access to customers' perceptions of competing products and services.

☐    The customers are able to provide an objective but informed judgement of how the business projects itself in the marketplace.

☐    Involving customers in the improvement discussions invites their participation in, and loyalty to, the business.

## Weaknesses

○    Customers cannot be expected to know or consider your strategy.

○    Customers tend to want 'much of the same except better' so may be limited in the amount of creative thinking they apply to questions.

○    Customers can be fickle; even if you give them what they say they want they may defect to someone who offers something better than they could ever have envisaged.

○    Customer expectations require skilful interpretation.

## Business objectives perspective

While benchmarking peripheral activities can provide useful learning opportunities, greater long-term benefit derives from benchmarking activities which link clearly to corporate or business objectives. Particularly in the lean organizations which constitute the rump of enterprise, little commitment or resources will be channelled towards initiatives or projects unless they demonstrably advance the purpose and intent of the firm.

Debating, discussing and agreeing such questions as those listed below are integral to the formulation of business objectives.

Benchmarking activity which enables the organization to achieve these will prove a substantial asset when communicating the rationale for benchmarking. It will also secure greater support and commitment across the 'body' of managers. Furthermore, it significantly influences attitudes and reactions to requests from benchmarking project leaders when they are recruiting team resources from parts of the organization over which they have no authority or control (Figure 2.7).

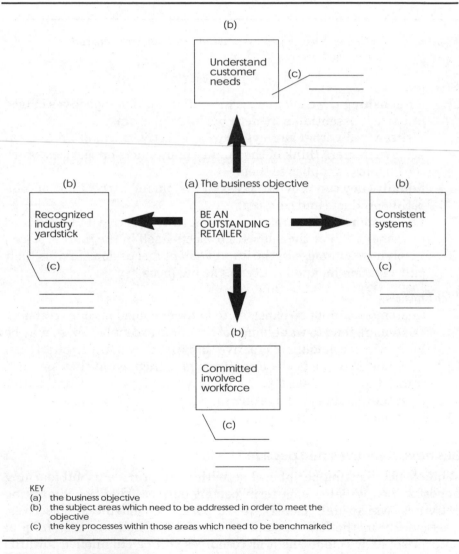

KEY
(a)  the business objective
(b)  the subject areas which need to be addressed in order to meet the objective
(c)  the key processes within those areas which need to be benchmarked

*Figure 2.7  Model showing business objectives identified by a retailing organization*

The following questions focus attention on objectives:

1.  What is/are the prime goal(s)/purpose(s) of the organization? ((a) in Figure 2.7)
2.  What has to be done to achieve this (these)? ((b) in Figure 2.7)
3.  What are the key processes in each of these areas? ((c) in Figure 2.7)
4.  Which are the priorities – short, medium and long term – in the context of achieving the objectives?
5.  Which process(es) should effort, therefore, be focused on in order to achieve these objectives?

*Strengths*
❐  Business priorities determine selection of benchmarking projects.
❐  The resultant improvements contribute towards attaining the overall objectives of the organization.
❐  The level of commitment to ensure the 'success' of benchmarking activity is likely to be higher if linked to achievement of business objectives, which in turn may be linked to personal objectives.

*Weaknesses*
○  May take time if the objectives have not been agreed or communicated.
○  May require outside facilitation to maintain objectivity.
○  Unless firmly prioritized, this approach could lead to attempts to benchmark too many processes at once which would tie-up more resource than may be practicable.

## Business excellence perspective

The European, and several national quality awards are based on a generic framework which organizes the activities of the firm into nine sections or areas of activity, five of which enable the achievement of results and four of which reflect the results of the various business activities. This has come to be known as the European Business Excellence Model (Figure 2.8).[5] Its comprehensive interpretation of business activities and purpose, coupled with adoption across Europe have been instrumental in its appeal to managers across the Community. Many are now using the self-assessment, which is integral to award submissions, as the basis for identifying areas of weakness. These subsequently become the 'subject' of continuous improvement and benchmarking projects, as previous winners have testified: 'Commitment to self-assessment and continuous improvement has increased our profitability' (Alan Jones, Managing Director,

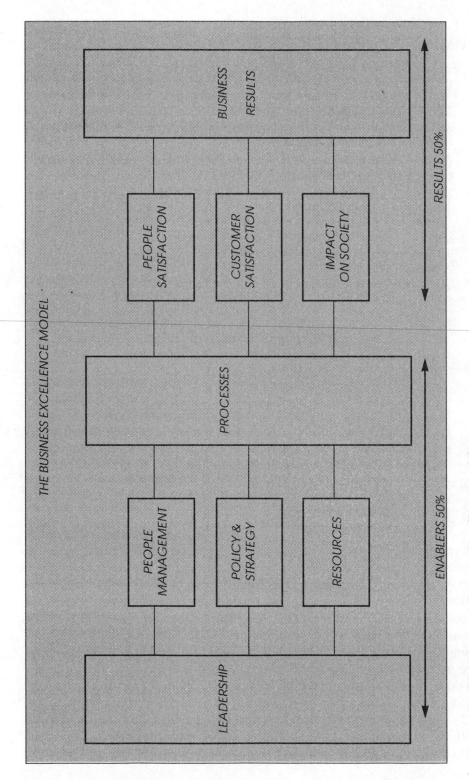

*Figure 2.8   The European Business Excellence model*

TNT Express (UK), UK Quality Award Winner for Business Excellence, 1994); 'You have to focus on business excellence to survive' (Keith Greenough, Managing Director, Mortgage Express UK Quality Award Winner for Business Excellence, 1996).

*Strengths*

☐ The commonality of approach and its adoption across a broad geographical base facilitates like-with-like performance comparison.

☐ Self-assessment against the criteria can highlight areas of relative strength and weakness in the enterprise.

☐ Relevant processes can then be benchmarked to minimize weaknesses and optimize strengths.

☐ Continuous self-assessment ultimately leads to improvement across the whole business.

*Weaknesses*

○ Performance comparison is based on relative current achievement.

○ Does not identify who the better performers are.

○ Necessitates long-term commitment.

○ May be difficult to prioritize benchmarking projects if several areas of weakness emerge.

## STEP 2: DEFINE THE PROCESS(ES)

Having decided the area in which to benchmark (for example, innovation, customer service, financial management), the next step involves identifying and defining the processes. Once you know which process (for example, capturing enquiries, telephone answering, paying accounts) you are going to focus on, you assemble the team, and begin to go through the following four stages of process definition shown in Figure 2.9.

### Define the boundaries

It does not matter where you set your boundaries, only that the team members understand, agree and work within the same ones. Do not attempt to take in too much the first time around. Start with manageable chunks while people are learning the technique so that (a) you finish the project, and (b) you have some positive results in a relatively short time (say, three to six months) to show for your efforts.

Table 2.1 indicates other questions which must be addressed at this stage.

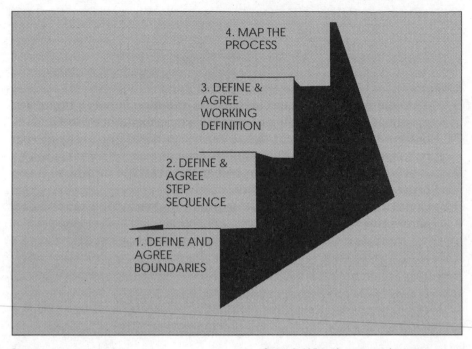

Step 1

◆ What is the output of the process?
◆ Who is the customer?
◆ What are the customer's requirements?
◆ Is this what the process delivers?
◆ Where does it begin?
◆ Where does it end?
◆ Who owns the process?

Step 2: What happens between the first and last step of the process? Involves those working in it. Construct the flow chart

Step 3: What is the objective of the process?

Step 4: Ultimately, combine the flow charts into a process map of the organization.

*Figure 2.9    Process definition steps*

## Agree what is happening between the first and last steps of the process

Involve the people who work in the process between the first and last steps as they have now been defined. Find out exactly what goes on by getting everyone together and working out what happens and why (this is not always the same as what is written in the procedures or quality manual).

Sticky notepads (such as 'Post-it'™ notes) can be invaluable when first sorting out the sequence of events. When you have identified the actual steps and the order in which they take place, you then link them

| Table 2.1   Setting the boundaries of the process | |
| --- | --- |
| *Boundary-setting questions* | *Associated questions* |
| What is the output of the process? | What exactly does it exist to produce? |
| Who is the customer? | Internal or external? Home, export, new, lapsed, key account? Each process has its own specific customer(s) |
| What does the customer require? | What specification has s/he given? Number, date and time of delivery, shape, size, colour, quality? |
| Is this what the process delivers? | What feedback mechanisms, procedures and measures exist to ensure that the customers' demands are being met? Are they being met at all? |
| If not, is the process necessary? | Does the process add value to the business if not to the customer? If not, why does it exist? |
| Where does the process begin? | What is the first step? For instance, in an order receiving process, is the first step when the salesman closes a deal or when the paperwork is received in the sales office? Or when the order is placed on the plant? |
| Where does the process end? | What is the final step? For instance, in the above process is it when the confirmation of order is sent to the customer, when goods are shipped to the warehouse, when they are despatched, or when they are received by the customer? |
| Who is the process owner? | Is there a named individual with authority and responsibility over the process? |

up into a 'flow chart' describing how they fit together. A simple example is provided in Figure 2.10. Standard conventions for the information shapes (such as decisions, data required, process steps) which are used for flow charting and apply across all industries are given in Figure 2.11. These ensure that charts can be interpreted by other people both in your own organization and those that are, or may become, future external benchmarking 'partners'.

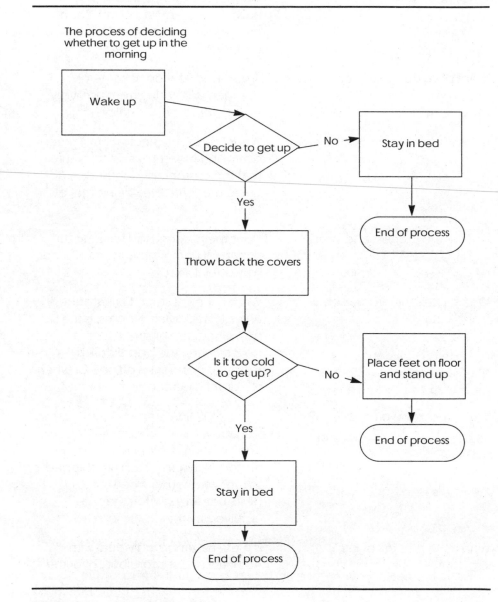

*Figure 2.10    Sample flow chart*

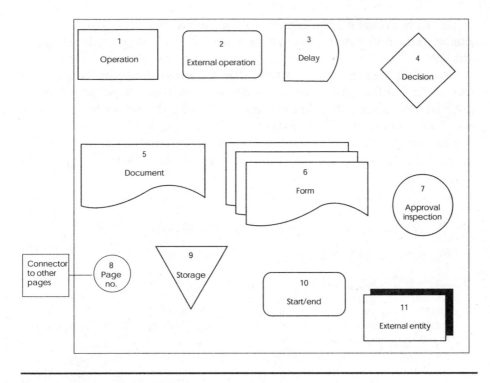

*Figure 2.11    Standard flow-charting conventions*

The flow chart will identify decisions, delays, repetitions (the same step is often repeated several times within a process – usually needlessly simply because nobody has noticed), feedback loops (often these do not exist and will need to be added in), and so forth. You should then agree which are the most important steps in the process and for each of these assign or devise measures of cost, quality and time according to the customer's requirements.

The flow chart rapidly clarifies why inefficiencies exist. People do what they do in the order they do them for any number of reasons, the most common of which are:

○    'it's the way it's always been done'
○    'it's the way I was taught'
○    'it's easier this way'.

Charting the flow of activities identifies which are being repeated needlessly, or too frequently. It also highlights where assumptions about what is happening are incorrect. It is not unusual, for example, to find out that something is not occurring at all, or is being done but at an inappropriate point.

The first 'returns' from benchmarking usually occur at this stage as waste, error and duplication are identified and, subsequently, stripped out.

An example of initial benefits realized through flow-charting is presented in Figure 2.12. The Royal Society for the Protection of Birds (RSPB) was among the first organizations in the charities sector to adopt benchmarking. One of the first areas targeted for attention was the finance function where a total of 144 processes was identified and systematically analysed for improvement opportunities. Figure 2.12 depicts the results.

---

FINANCE FUNCTION BENCHMARKING BENEFITS REALIZED

144 processes identified, 99 mapped, 25 reviewed:

- 43 days labour saved
- 33 000 sheets A4 paper eliminated
- £3 000 unrecovered VAT identified and recovered
- Intangible benefits in Security, Health & Safety and Audit Compliance: training made easier and better assimilated

*Source*: Reproduced courtesy of Royal Society for the Protection of Birds, Sandy, Bedfordshire, UK 1997

---

*Figure 2.12    Benchmarking in charities*

## Agree a common working definition for the process

This should be a clear description of what the process objective is; for example, 'responding to every external customer enquiry within two working days' as opposed to 'responding promptly to customer queries'.

Test whether you have a clear working definition by showing it around to people who are not involved in the team's project. Do they understand exactly what you are getting at? If so, fine: if not, redefine. This descriptive definition will be used in discussions with potential partners. Will it be clear to them what you are talking about? It pays to spend time at this early stage clarifying and checking understanding.

As President Nixon is attributed as having said during the 1974 Watergate investigations: 'I know you think you understand what you think I said, but I'm not sure you realize that what you think you heard is not really what I meant.'

## Map the process

Flow charts are the everyday working mechanics for describing processes. As you progress to benchmarking numerous processes, the cumulative flow charts link with each other to provide a graphic description, or picture, of the relationship between these processes. In a sense, process maps are akin to world maps. We all have an idea of where countries or continents fit in relation to each other, but it is not so easy to describe accurately where, for instance, towns are in relation to each other. Is Berlin north or south of London? Is Paris further west than Lisbon, or Johannesburg further east than Harare? We may guess, but having a world map makes it absolutely clear.

Likewise process maps. However, since the resultant picture is a series of lines and different shaped boxes, these bear more resemblance to automotive wiring diagrams than geographical maps. Their strength is that they portray clearly what the organization does, as well as the interrelationships and distances between what happens and where, in the firm. Furthermore, the map provides a comprehensive but uncluttered picture. The full detail of what happens in the individual processes can be stored in a computer, accessible through keying in certain reference numbers provided on the map.

## STEP 3 IDENTIFY POTENTIAL PARTNERS

Process definition in Step 2 (see Figure 2.9) will highlight the opportunities for improvement. It may immediately be possible to identify necessary actions to achieve this. However, it is equally likely that the solution may not be obvious and it will be necessary to find someone elsewhere who can help. Alternatively, you may simply feel that 'there must be a better way to do this' and will want to seek better practice elsewhere. Hence, Step 3 involves identifying potential 'partners' whom you could learn from and who might indicate ways to optimize the opportunities uncovered through the previous step.

You may know who to go to, or you may not. Assuming the latter, set up a creative brainstorming session for the team based on the following questions: Who is most likely to be good at this (process or process step which needs to be improved)? Who has to do this well to stay in business? Consider any industry, organization or enterprise. The list should include about 20 names of potential 'better performing' organizations who could be approached as partners. Make sure there is a mix of possibilities; some local, others distant, a few less obvious than the rest and even one or two really long shots. Think of different industries and sectors where the process is crucial or highly important. Also think about similar but unrelated processes where some of the same criteria might apply. For example, seeking to improve its vacancy-filling process the Employment Services benchmarking team listed a major supermarket chain as a potential partner in the anticipation that they might learn something from the latter's shelf-filling process. Their thinking is clearly explained in the case study in the final chapter of this book.

Partners are referred to as 'internal' if they are found within your organization, regardless of whether they are at the same or a different location. For instance, if you were benchmarking the telephone answering aspect of the customer service process, you may find many potential partners with better practices within your organization or group of companies.

When cooperation is sought with others outside your firm, the partners are referred to as 'external' regardless of whether they are in the same industry or not. Thus, for instance, if you were interested in improving the performance throughout your supply chain, it might be necessary to look for partners in other firms who could be in your own industry or a totally different sector, depending on where measurably better practices were found to exist.

Since mind blocks and group thinking can be difficult to recognize from within the team, you may find it useful to employ a professional facilitator for the 'potential partner' brainstorming session. It may be better to employ someone from outside your firm as they will not be bound by your culture and constraints, nor prone to 'this is the way we always do things' thinking (sometimes referred to as the not-invented-here (or nih) syndrome). Many firms have realized the benefit of this approach (Rank Xerox, TI Group, British Steel, for example) and have trained their own in-house facilitators who are able to be deployed across the business regardless of location. The benefit of this approach, apart from savings on the cost of employing outside experts, is that such facilitators have a sound understanding of the business, which can be helpful in supplying a contextual framework for the brainstorming.

Firms often consider themselves to be 'unique' in terms of the sphere of their operations. This can squash new ideas because, the thinking goes, 'if it was not invented here it will not work'. However, lateral and creative thinking need to become a way of life if the intention is to out-smart your competitive opponents.

## Step 4: Data sources and collection

The objective of this step is to identify and plan where to find data on the organizations who emerge from the brainstorming of the previous step. The team need enough data to inform them which of the potential partners are definite possibilities and which are distinct rejects. There is an almost inexhaustible amount of data available to those who look for it. Generally speaking, 95 per cent of what you need is already available in the public domain. So it is wise to base the search on criteria which will enable the appropriate amount of data to be found, keep the search time to a minimum and avoid the team becoming inundated with unnecessary material.

You may prefer to set the criteria before the brainstorming in Step 3. However, they could then act as too firm a brake on creative thinking. A solution to this dilemma is to repeat the brainstorming exercise before and after drawing up the criteria, which might include:

O    *Location* – you may initially wish to restrict your activity to just one region or country; for instance in initial external benchmarking projects you may wish to visit a locally based firm to cut down on travel time and costs.

O    *Size* – you may decide to start with partners of a similar size to your own firm, or wish to find, for example, two the same, two much larger and two much smaller.

O    *Perceived organizational culture* – if seeking radical change you may decide to look at cultures totally different from yours (for example Employment Services considering supermarkets during their vacancy filling project).

O    *Ease of access* – will the potential partners want to talk to you? Some organizations on the list could prove difficult to approach. How long will you persevere? What have you got to offer in return in such instances?

Consider where and how to get the data which will enable you to match the potential list of partners against the criteria. Then plan who is to be responsible for gathering information, allocate budget and time constraints and commence the collection procedure. At this point you may decide to involve an outside 'expert' to collect the data and the best 'first port of call' is to contact your local Benchmarking Centre. In many cases this will prove a more efficient and effective way of searching for data than involving hard-pressed or inexperienced internal staff (Figure 2.13).

Keep the following points in mind:

O    you need enough data on the potential partner firms to indicate whether they meet your criteria or not

O    you should be aiming to reduce your initial list of potential partners to a maximum of seven names

O    these are the ones you will need to get more detailed information on in order to validate whether they remain on the potential list or are rejected

| Internal | External |
| --- | --- |
| Company library | National Libraries |
| Corporate publications | Business School Libraries |
| Company databases | External databases |
| Customer Surveys | National Surveys |
| Market research | Trade shows, journals |
| Personal networks | Media reports, analysts |
| New employees | Finance houses |
| Non-executive Directors | Suppliers, customers |
| Intranet | Trade Associations |
| | National Press |
| | Press cuttings Agencies |
| | Benchmarking Centres |
| | National Quality Institutes |
| | Universities, Business schools |
| | Professional Institutes |
| | Company reports |
| | Seminars, conferences, etc. |
| | Professional networks |
| | Award bodies |
| | Internet |

*Figure 2.13    Data sources: Useful starting points*

O   those which remain (aim for three to five) are the ones who will be
     approached verbally or face to face to gather any final information
     on which to base your final partner choice.

## SUMMARY OF THE FIRST STAGE

Planning is the most crucial part of any successful activity. It ensures
that:

O   the events which follow proceed as desired and expected
O   eventualities are covered so that the inevitable surprises, that is,
     all those unforeseen factors which always occur, are manageable
     and
O   their impact on activities which follow can be seen and relevant
     additional or alternative actions can be initiated.

The first stage is also the most important one for as many as possible of
the team to be fully involved in. Including them will ensure they are all
aware of the detail of the project being undertaken. From this point on,
however, team members may be involved in individual tasks, for

example, data gathering may be done by just one or perhaps two members. Nor will the whole team need to attend site visits.

So, before moving into the second stage of the methodology the team should have a project debriefing session to ensure that:

O    everyone fully understands the objectives
O    shares the same vision, and
O    is sure of their position and role for what follows.

Time spent in confirmation and repetition at this point will be more than repaid through enabling the project to proceed with minimum misunderstanding and confusion.

Once everyone is absolutely sure they understand these factors the next stage of the project – analysis – can be undertaken. This is the focus of the next chapter.

## NOTES

1    Taken from a paper entitled 'Facilitating and supporting best practices to achieve business excellence' by C. Dabadie, Quality Manager, TI France – Business Intelligence Conference 1997.
2    For the full background to this model see Codling, S. (1995), *Best Practice Benchmarking: The Management Guide*, Aldershot: Gower.
3    Chief Executive, Lew Platt, quoted in *Financial Times*, 18.3.94.
4    'Dynamics of best practice' Brian S. Codling, *Benchmarking for Quality Management & Technology*, **4** (2), 96–103.
5    Full details available from the British Quality Foundation and the European Foundation for Quality Management (see Appendix 2: Useful contacts).

CHAPTER

# 3

# THE ANALYSIS STAGE

## BENCHMARKING METHODOLOGY: SECOND STAGE – ANALYSIS

The analysis stage of the methodology moves the benchmarking project *from* the point at which team members start to analyse the gathered data on other organizations, or other parts of your own organization, according to the broad criteria selected in Step 4, *to* the point at which recommendations are made regarding the targets at which improvement activities could or should be aimed (Figure 3.1).

At this stage your team should include someone who is experienced in using such problem solving tools as histograms, fish-bone analyses and Pareto charts.[1] These will be invaluable in 'showing' the size of performance gap and potential opportunities for improvement. It is also during this stage that the 'devil's advocate'[2] becomes involved if you need to make a site visit.

THE BENCHMARKING PROCESS

*The analysis stage*

5  Collect the data and select partners
6  Determine the performance gap
7  Establish the difference in the process
8  Target future performance

*Figure 3.1   Second stage steps of benchmarking methodology*

The following four steps, Steps 5–8 inclusive, enable the project to move through this stage.

## STEP 5: ANALYSE DATA AND SELECT PARTNERS

Step 4 enabled you to plan and commence collecting data in order to eliminate the obviously unsuitable firms from your list of potential partners. During Step 5, the data is examined more closely and compared critically against the selection criteria. At this point you may decide more detailed information is required on some of the organizations in order to help the selection process. It should be possible to collect this without making direct contact. If this is not the case, however, it is wise to use a third party initially for gathering the information to avoid prejudicing any future cooperation.

When all the necessary information has been gathered, sifted and analysed a short list of most likely potential partners must be drawn up. The team should then compile a list of broadly pertinent questions which will be used as a conversational aid over the telephone when making the first contact or sent direct to a named person in the target organization.

The following points should be kept in mind:

1.  the questionnaire in this context is a concise, focused tool which will inform and guide future discussions. It is not a general market research document with numerous pages and endless multi-choice options
2.  it should be short – 12–15 questions is a good working average but certainly no more than 20
3.  it should help determine whether the target is a suitable partner from which to learn how to improve your process
4   do not include any questions on which you would not provide reciprocal information
5.  send as much information with the questionnaire to the target company as will enable the recipient to understand where you are coming from – such as who you are, what you have done so far and why you think they can help
6.  include a copy of *The Benchmarking Code of Conduct*[3]
7.  if the initial questionnaire confirms the feasibility of going ahead, it may be necessary to draw up a supplementary and perhaps more detailed questionnaire for use during your visit.

Figures 3.2, 3.3 and 3.4 provide an example of how one company tackled their questionnaire. James Dawson & Son Limited are a medium-sized enterprise (roughly 270 employees) who supply rubber hose products to the automotive industry. Their first benchmarking project focused on the management and continuous improvement monitoring of suppliers. The questionnaires in the figure below were drawn up following their identification of a potential local benchmarking partner (a dairy). Figure 3.2 was mailed to the dairy's Chief Executive Officer with additional information, as shown, following an initial telephone contact. The responses prompted the questions in 3.3 which, in turn, led to development of the questionnaire in 3.4, which formed the basis of the discussions during a single site visit.

| CRITERIA FOR POTENTIAL PARTNER SELECTION | QUESTION | ANSWER |
|---|---|---|
| 1 | Do you have a supplier management system? | Yes |
| 2 | How big is your supplier base (approx.) | 12 suppliers |
| 3 | Number of materials purchased (approx.) | Range of approx. 300 |
| 4 | Supplier assessment period/ frequency? | Annual |
| 5 | What is your supplier assessment criteria? | As per audit or audit questionnaire |
| 6 | How is your data gathered: manual or computer? | Computer |
| 7 | How many people are involved with supplier control and data capture? | 10 |
| 8 | Do you have a process map? | Yes |
| 9 | What are your supplier defect costs? | Unknown but suspect low |
| 10 | How do you control supplier reaction to defect concerns:<br>a) steps taken<br><br>b) timescale<br><br><br>c) verification | a) Contact supplier direct and report incidents to CMTA* committee auditor<br>b) Suppliers discussed at every technical committee meeting every eight weeks<br>c) By CMTA auditor who follows up complaints on behalf of the committee<br>*Cooperative Milk Trade Association |
| 11 | Do you have a supplier development programme? | In the case of milk, yes; others vary |

*Figure 3.2    Benchmarking questionnaire*

| CRITERIA FOR POTENTIAL PARTNER SELECTION | QUESTION | ANSWER |
|---|---|---|
| 12 | How, and how often, do you communicate with your supplier base – meetings, phone, fax? | With most we communicate daily; with packaging it varies |
| 13 | What criteria do you use to choose your suppliers? | CMTA approval |
| 14 | What techniques do you use to improve supplier performance? | Quality Analysis |
| 15 | Do you monitor customer feedback? | Yes |
| 16 | What is your major customer | Doorstep milk deliveries |
| 17 | Would you be willing to establish a major contact/name for this project? | Yes |

*Notes*:
Annexe to questionnaire:
James Dawson benchmarking contacts:
Managing Director     – Benchmarking Executive Champion
Commercial Director    – Benchmarking Project Leader
Purchasing Manager    – Benchmarking Project Coordinator
Quality Manager       – Benchmarking Facilitator
Receptionist         – Benchmarking Team Member

Attachments to questionnaire:
(i)    Benchmarking code of conduct
(ii)   Synopsis of Benchmarking
(iii)  Examples of supplier process measures as supplied by DTI/BRMA

*Source*: Reproduced with kind permission of James Dawson & Son Limited

---

*Figure 3.2    Benchmarking questionnaire (concluded)*

| QUESTION | COMMENT/ANSWER |
|---|---|
| 1 Do we have synergy? Fit? | Synergy (Yes)<br>Fit????? |
| 2 They have a limited supplier base? | These are approved by the CMTA |
| 3 They do not monitor supplier cost? | Unknown and low |
| 4 Suppliers reaction to defects? | Person to person follow up checked by CMTA audit |
| 5 Supplier development programme? | Milk (Yes) but would this fit in with the proactive requirements of the automotive industry (QS9000)? |
| 6 Comprehensive data base programme that can analyse all deliveries, defects etc.? | Without major expenditure would this fit in with our paper system? |

*Source*: Reproduced with kind permission of James Dawson & Son Limited

**Figure 3.3    *Questions raised by the questionnaire***

QUESTIONS

1    What criteria does the CMTA use to approve suppliers?

2    How does the CMTA control supplier defect concerns:
    – What steps are taken?
    – Timescale?
    – Verification?

3    In-depth analysis of measures used to monitor suppliers:
Our measures are:  (a)  Delivery performance
                (b)  Quality performance
                (c)  Order/invoice accuracy
                (d)  Response to quality concerns

4    Is customer feedback/satisfaction monitored?

5    Are suppliers issued with a hard copy of general quality guidelines?

*Source*: Reproduced with kind permission of James Dawson & Son Limited

**Figure 3.4    *Questions for further discussion***

## STEP 6: DETERMINE THE SIZE OF THE GAP

Up to this point you have made your selection of the partner firm on the basis of data you have gathered. This will have suggested that they are performing better at whichever process is the subject of your improvement efforts. During this step, the objective is to establish the magnitude of difference. This may, or may not, necessitate a site visit but if it does you should aim to incorporate both the determination of the gap (the focus of Step 7) and the process differences which may be responsible for it (Step 8).

In order to determine the nature and size of the gap you will need to compare measurements of the same things in the same, or similar, process. Discussions with the partnering firm may show that although some parts of your process are less effective than theirs (what is known as a negative gap) other parts of it perform better (which results in a positive gap). One of the benefits to them could be learning from such positive gaps how to improve their process still further. It will certainly help in your approach to them if you have found this out beforehand.

You will have mapped your process and defined the critical performance measures and will share this information with the benchmarking partner. If they have similarly mapped their process, comparison will be relatively easy. For instance, if your map (say, for paying regular customer invoices) involves 23 steps over a period of nine days, whereas the partner does it in 12 steps within three days, you could rapidly identify where the differences, or opportunities for improvement, lay.

In many cases, however, the firm you have approached will not have mapped the particular process as you are 'looking' at it. Hence, a detailed discussion will be required. Any site visit for that purpose should include the right people from the right part of the process carried out in the other firm otherwise you may not get sufficiently detailed information. It is important to clarify this with your hosts at the time the visit is organized. In some cases, the company may be sufficiently interested to take the time to map their process (if they have not already done so) and the help you are able to provide them, in theory and practice, may provide an excellent return benefit to them.

## STEP 7: ESTABLISH PROCESS DIFFERENCES

In Step 6 the existence of a performance gap was confirmed. Step 7 establishes the reasons or practices behind this. What do the better performing organizations do and why? If you have a clearly defined process map to show them they will more readily understand what you are doing. If theirs is not mapped you may have to take some time to help them with it (as indicated in Step 6) or wait while they produce it themselves, if they are willing to do so.

If you do not have the internal resource to do this, help may be called in from outside. Although this may sound like an unnecessary expense, weighing up the opportunity cost of your people, their time and the work they will have to set aside for the time it takes to help the other firm, will help to judge whether it is worthwhile.

'Why should they bother to do extra work to help us?' is an obvious question. Many organizations will ask this when you first approach them. So it is important to think through what can be offered in return for the help you are seeking from them. The possibility that your process might have a positive gap which the host firm could benefit from was covered in Step 6. Alternatively, is there an area where you are better than them and will you trade information on the process(es) concerned? If not, is it possible to teach them about process improvement, quality tools or other techniques which could benefit their business?

In some cases, it will be obvious when comparing maps that the host organization are engaged in a much shorter process. In other cases, it may be longer yet still more effective than your own.

Culture and tradition in firms have a major influence on why people perform better and many of your questions may need to be directed at these areas, rather than the process itself. While listening to the responses, be prepared to assess critically whether the way they do things is the way you *could* do things.

This may force you to face some hard facts. The cultural differences may be too great and there may be insufficient commitment in your organization to effect the degree of change required to introduce or support the best practice.

Alternatively, it may be that the time and cost required to make the change are greater than originally envisaged, planned or budgeted for. Such factors should prompt a review of the situation with a possible redrawing of the project objectives and/or timetable.


## STEP 8: TARGET FUTURE PERFORMANCE

By now you should have a detailed understanding of the size and nature of the gap in performance and what you need to do in your firm to improve process effectiveness and efficiency. Weighing this up against the resource, cultural and time considerations should enable you to devise targets which are realistic for your organization. It is wise when considering the time that will be required to achieve your targets, to allow at least 50 per cent extra for contingencies which may arise and interrupt or disrupt your schedules.

Good project planning and management become even more vital at this point. If you have a schedule with clearly described targets and milestones you will be able to communicate more effectively with the rest of the organization. Implementation will follow more smoothly as a result.

The project plan should include analysis of full resource details such as who is to do what, when, how much it will cost and how long will it take. Analysis such as this will provide a sound basis for the relevant managers to understand and judge the implications of the action plans and recommendations which arise from this second stage of the benchmarking activity. Without such detailed analysis, many benchmarking 'projects' fail.

## SUMMARY OF SECOND STAGE – ANALYSIS

As at the end of the first stage (planning), it is wise to debrief with the entire team before moving into the third stage of the project. The need for a project report and who will be responsible for writing it will become clear from this. Depending on the nature of the activity and organization, it may also be necessary for a presentation to be devised for, and made to, the project sponsor(s) before moving into the third stage. This should also be discussed and agreed during this session.

The project leader should be quite clear who is to be involved in the next phase of activities and have ensured that they will be available as and when they are required.

Once the analysis stage is completed and the above factors have been covered the project should be robust to move into its third stage and this 'implementation and action' is the subject of the next chapter.

## NOTES

1   Referred to as 'the tools of quality', details can be found in much of the literature on Total Quality Management or Statistical Process Control.
2   Defined by the *Penguin English Dictionary* (1965 edn) as 'one who argues to the contrary for the sake of debate'.
3   Available from benchmarking centres in UK and Europe (see Appendix 2 Useful contacts).

# ACTION AND IMPLEMENTATION STAGE

## BENCHMARKING METHODOLOGY: THIRD STAGE – ACTION

This stage is where the painstaking work of the previous two begins to pay dividends (Figure 4.1). Implementation of action plans arising out of the analysis of better performing processes should always be the goal from the outset of the benchmarking project. Whether or not this effectively materializes is a combination of diligence during the first two stages and rigorous monitoring and attention to detail during the third stage.

The four steps which are described below enable the process and ultimately the organization, as an increasing number of benchmarking initiatives are carried out, to move from where it is now to where its potential for competitive advantage is realized and the crucial 'edge' is gained.

---

THE BENCHMARKING PROCESS

*The action stage*

  9  Communication and commitment
 10  Adjust goals and develop improvement plan
 11  Implement and monitor

*Review*

 12  Review progress and re-calibrate

---

*Figure 4.1    Third stage steps of benchmarking methodology*

## STEP 9: COMMUNICATION

'I know you think you understand what you think I said, but I'm not sure you realize that what you think you heard is not really what I meant' (attributed to President Nixon, Watergate 1974).

Clear, effective and convincing communication is essential to the success of every project and benchmarking is no different (Figure 4.2). The objective is to enable recommendations to be understood by everyone and acceptance to be secured from those who are most affected by, or involved in, any changes.

The debriefing session at the end of the second stage will have identified or confirmed who is to be involved in ensuring that implementation is carried forward.

A team leader, or improvement manager, will be required to oversee and monitor the activities. This does not always have to be the most obvious person and, particularly if benchmarking is still new to the company, may be someone totally outside the process being improved. To achieve organizational buy-in to new techniques over the long term, it is important that initial projects are successful. Hence, it may be wise to identify a team leader for championing and implementing recommendations who is different from the person responsible in the first two stages.

The composition of the team will also alter to reflect the emphasis on improvement activity, with planners and information specialists being replaced by people working daily in the process.

Rank Xerox's Office Document Products Group, for instance, recognized that long-term buy-in to the practicalities of sharing best practices was reliant on the success of early projects. Selection of the managers responsible for implementation was based on their ability to push things through and get things done even if that meant 'importing' people from other parts of the business. Selection criteria included:

- youth
- flexibility
- ambition
- results orientation
- good organization skills and above all
- 'winning' attitudes.

Such people need to be identified and communicated with as early as possible so that they are ready and able to take up their new positions as soon as possible when the time comes.

## COMMUNICATIONS PLAN

DESCRIPTION OF THE VISION:

THE BENCHMARKING PARTNER

.............................................

.............................................

.............................................

Why selected:.......................................

THE PROCESS IMPROVEMENT TO HELP ACHIEVE

.......................................................

THIS:....................................

.......................................................

.............................................

.......................................................

THE BENCHMARKING TEAM:    .......................................................

.......................................................................................................

WHO WILL BE MOST AFFECTED BY IMPROVEMENT: .............................................................

..........................................................................................................................

WHO ELSE NEEDS/OUGHT TO KNOW?: ...........................................................................

..........................................................................................................................

| WHO: TARGET GROUPS          1 | 2 | 3 | 4 |
| --- | --- | --- | --- |
| Add further groups if necessary | | | |
| WHAT: | | | |
| Should each be made aware of? | | | |
| HOW: | | | |
| Are they going to react? Can they be included? | | | |
| WHAT: | | | |
| Will be method of communication? | | | |
| WHO: | | | |
| Will be responsible? | | | |
| WHEN: | | | |
| Will communication take place? | | | |
| REVIEW DATES: | | | |
| EFFECTIVENESS MEASURES | | | |

*Figure 4.2    A communications plan template*

Figure 4.2 provides a simple template for developing communications. It enables you to consider the messages you may need to get across to the different individuals and groups together with the delivery mechanisms and timing for them.

A section for 'effectiveness measures' is included at the bottom of the template. The following questions will provide food for thought when considering these:

O    What percentage of the target audience should the message reach?
O    Within what period should this be achieved?
O    How will the means of getting the message across be measured?
O    What feedback mechanisms will be set up?
O    How often will these be monitored?
O    Who will be responsible for measurement?
O    How much authority will be vested in that person for altering the message or the medium?
O    Is there a budget for this activity?
O    How will 'value for money' be identified?

Ideally, a plan such as that suggested in the template should be built in to the benchmarking project from the outset. Although when you start it is not possible to know what you are going to find or what the recommendations for improvement action are going to be, the discipline will prompt the team to consider regularly those who need to be kept informed along with how and when this might best be achieved.

Communication from the team to the organization should also encourage the ideas to flow in the corresponding direction. This will afford opportunities for comments and contributions from the broad constituency. Additionally, it may influence acceptance and buy-in by those not directly involved in the project who will nevertheless be affected by its recommendations.

Furthermore, as the communications programme begins to penetrate across the firm it will become clear whether or not the targets set in Step 8 are realistically achievable. It is often the case that these have to be amended in the light of other people's agenda, priorities and budgets which only emerge during the broad communications process. However, it is important to encourage such potential difficulties to emerge as they will impact on the activities in the subsequent step.

## STEP 10: ADJUST YOUR TARGETS AND DEVISE THE IMPROVEMENT IMPLEMENTATION PLAN

As you start getting feedback from your communication plan you will develop a feel for the accuracy and suitability of your original targets.

During this step any adjustments to these should be made and incorporated in the final improvement project implementation plan. This should show the desired state (for the process) at an identified future date, together with the essential steps for achieving it. Milestones and objectives should be stated in the plan, the totality of which must then be incorporated in the rolling communications programme across the organization.

The improvements will inevitably mean doing things differently, or doing different things, which, equally unavoidably, will take more time, effort and thought − at least until familiarity is achieved. Ultimately, the process will be more effective and efficient which means that those involved in it will have this initial investment repaid.

However, since the end state will not necessarily be obvious or convincing at the outset, the project manager should ensure at this point that the individuals involved in implementation have clear personal objectives linked to those for the process improvement. If these individuals have not been involved up to this point, their managers will need to be consulted and involved in the objectives development process. Furthermore, personal and process objectives should be linked clearly to those of the organization and the senior managers must be comfortable with these linkages.

Implementation will be more or less successful depending on the degree of commitment to change and improvement on the part of all those involved in the process chain. However, success will also be determined by attention to the detail and follow-through on actions. Building these factors into the plan is the prime responsibility of the benchmarking project manager.

## STEP 11: IMPLEMENTATION

By this stage in the project, a considerable number of people will have been involved from your organization and that of the partner if you have needed to look outside for comparable processes. Between three and 18 months will have elapsed since the outset; financial and other resources will have been deployed.

Implementation may not always be easy. Changing the way things are done inevitably courts resistance. Nevertheless, it is arguably the only justification for this use of resource. Certainly future benchmarking projects undertaken in the organization will be judged by the degree of improvement or amount of saving attributed to previous exercises.

Although there are no magic formulae for successful implementation, unfailing attention to detail and rigorous follow-through are the hallmarks. The project manager is responsible for monitoring progress against milestones and deadlines via regular review sessions with the implementation team. Regular communication of progress and success in achieving targets will secure interest and the commitment of the rest of the organization.

The project manager plays a vital part at this stage in liaising between the project champion or sponsor and the process owner. It is his or her continuing role to keep the 'top team' informed of the success and savings gained through benchmarking in order to maintain their commitment and active support. It should also stand the organization in good stead for securing funding for future improvement projects.

Old hands at benchmarking, such as TI Group, Rover, Motorola, ICL and Hewlett Packard did not initiate benchmarking as part of their culture overnight. In some cases it took a number of years before they could reflect, with the benefit of hindsight, on how useful the technique had been to them and what the actual payback on the bottom line amounted to.

Although visible returns may be achieved within a shorter time-frame, it will not necessarily be easy to allocate precise financial savings to these until a cumulative or critical mass of improvements has had time to work through the company. Knock-on effects from introducing process improvements are equally hard to quantify. These may include such factors as individuals feeling more 'valued' as a result of taking part in the process improvement, or clutter being removed from the workplace as processes are 'cleaned up'. While these undoubtedly enhance the quality of working life, it would be almost impossible to ascribe financial values to them.

This is all the more reason for knowing what the process involved – in terms of cost and resource – at the outset of the project. With that marker firmly in place, it is possible at any future stage to compare current figures. Rather like a saving scheme; it may not sound much to start with, but as time passes and interest is added, it can add up to a substantial total. Eventually, enhancements to working life will work through customer satisfaction ratings, at which stage the financial gains will be measurable in for instance, repeat or recommended business.

## STEP 12: REVIEW AND RECYCLE

Once the implementation plan has been followed through the entire team, including the project sponsor, should get together to review progress against objectives. By this stage, the process should have reached the level of performance that was targeted. Certain questions therefore need to be addressed. These include:

○   Is the process now the 'best' it can be?
○   If so, what actions are needed to maintain this state?
○   Who is responsible for these actions?
○   If the process is not the 'best' it can be, should 'new' comparators be found from whom we can incorporate other ideas and additional learning?
○   Does this involve the same, or a new benchmarking team?
○   What has been learned from the project?
○   How should this be communicated to others, both in the organization and outside it?
○   What were the main learning points and pitfalls that need to be factored in when you start the next project?
○   How will these be communicated to others?
○   Have you signed things off with the partnering organization, updating them fully on your progress and actions?
○   Does the partner wish to stay in contact on this, or for a future, project?

After a few projects and iterations of the methodology, familiarity with the steps to be followed will have spread across the organization. A common language will have developed and people in different parts of the firm may well express a need or intention to initiate benchmarking projects. It is not unusual for firms to gradually evolve their own in-house benchmarking methodology which, though based on the preceding recommended steps, will bear the hallmarks of their own unique culture and way of doing things. In this way, TNT Express (UK) have evolved a five-step process, Xerox have a ten-step process, AT&T have an eight-step process and one firm in the automotive sector at one stage had a 35-step process.

In effect, the number of steps is immaterial. What matters is that projects are carefully planned, that your own processes are thoroughly analysed and understood before any partners are approached and that reasonable actions are implemented to secure the improvement opportunities identified. Ultimately, benchmarking will lead to visible improvements in your firm's performance and overall competitiveness.

## SUMMARY OF THE THIRD STAGE

During the third stage, the necessary activities are carried out which ensure that the process being focused on becomes the 'best' it can be or meets the objectives identified in the project plan. Since it may take several repetitions of the benchmarking cycle before the ultimate 'best' state is achieved, the end of the third stage need not necessarily mark the end of the benchmarking project. Hence, at this point a team debriefing is required to review the overall position.

Factors which will need to be considered during this session include:

○ Is the project to continue?
○ Who is to be responsible for overseeing the project?
○ Does this require an extended, or a new project plan?
○ When is the next review session to be held?
○ Is liaison with the partner(s) continuing?
○ If so, what actions are being taken?
○ Who is responsible?
○ What are the arrangements for transferring the learning across the organization generally and other benchmarking teams specifically?

If the third stage debrief shows that the project has met all its objectives then it should be signed off. Congratulate and reward the team for their efforts and ensure that appropriate communications regarding the end of the project are actioned.

When a few projects have been conducted it should be possible to extract and document the learning points about how benchmarking works across your organization. It is important to capture and communicate these so that those involved in future projects benefit from the knowledge and learning and do not 'reinvent wheels'.

Now the task, considered in detail in Chapter 6, will be determination of who is to be responsible for overall coordination of the firms' improvement benchmarking activities .

However, before looking at the long-term implications it is well to consider some of the benefits which will derive from rigorously following the methodology outlined in the preceding pages. This, then, is the focus of the next chapter.

CHAPTER

# 5

# WHAT ARE THE BENEFITS?

Benchmarking is often linked in the public perception with large, profitable organizations. Certainly many of these – Motorola, Rank Xerox, TI, Rover Group, Rolls Royce – do use the technique but it is arguable whether they are successful because they are benchmarking or benchmark because they are profitable.

Table 5.1 provides a list which represents the benefits which will become apparent as a result of introducing benchmarking. Some of the factors included in this table merit further explanation.

## IMPROVED PERFORMANCE AND PROFITABILITY

Increased profitability is the motive for most improvement activity. However, the benefits from benchmarking also come through in several areas which are 'intangible'. It may be a while before financial benefits show up on the bottom line and can be linked to profitability. Although it may be difficult to isolate exactly how much is saved through benchmarking activities alone, some companies such as Shell Exploration and Trading have identified figures as high as £50 million (in their 1996 European Best Practice Benchmarking Award™-winning case study), whilst Rank Xerox suggest a figure of $US600 million in their Office Documents Products Group and Texas Instruments reckoned to save the cost of building a new plant – approximately $US500 million – in two successive years through facilitated sharing of internal best practices and a total of $US1.3 billion in almost three years. In the charities sector, the Royal Society for the Protection of Birds identified £500 000 savings as a result of benchmarking their purchasing process.

| Table 5.1    Benefits to the organization as a result of benchmarking | | |
|---|---|---|
| **Benefit** | **How** | **When** |
| Improved performance and profitability | Improving efficiency and effectiveness of processes reduces costs associated with waste and reworking errors | Initially when processes are analysed; continuing throughout the 'life' of benchmarking in the firm |
| Clarity of leadership | Discussion on what improvement would bring biggest benefit | Prior to starting the project |
| Clarity of management and enhanced communication | Focus on key processes helps manage where it matters | In first three months |
| Saving or better utilization of resources | Analysing processes and finding out exactly what is going on | In first three months |
| Increased efficiency of operations | Remove error, rework and duplication in processes | In first three months |
| Greater value creation or reduction of non-value adding activities | Questioning which activities in the process add value and eliminating those which do not | In first three months |
| Challenge current thinking | Learning from others' mistakes saves time and speeds up the learning curve. Also increases speed of learning about new things in the organization | When networks are accessed or potential partners contacted – ongoing |
| External focus and tapping into innovations in other sectors/countries | During data search and collection/networking for information | Begins within first three months but becomes evident within 12 |
| Reduces fire-fighting and improves quality of working life | As processes become more efficient and effective | Gradually from month 1 onwards |
| Beneficial impact on customers and suppliers | By taking their perspective and views into account as you tighten up processes | Gradually from the first month onwards |
| Opens doors to other organizations | The technique provides a purpose and common language | As external benchmarking progresses |

The message which comes through from such examples is that you must have an indicative cost of the process at the outset, that is, before any improvement action is taken. Even if the figure is not precise, it will provide a marker against which to evaluate future measurements, hence enabling the savings to be estimated.

## CLARITY OF LEADERSHIP AND MANAGEMENT

The 'intangible' benefits usually become apparent long before the financial savings begin to be revealed. Clarity of leadership and management is a major outcome, brought about through the intense focus on key issues, objectives and processes coupled with the means of improving these.

The daily focus is on what is important and eliminating what is ineffective or unnecessary. Fire-fighting becomes a thing of the past as processes become more efficient and, with the focus increasingly on delivering what the customer needs, relationships at that end of the chain are also improved. Cutting out the fire-fighting makes a significant difference to individual's productivity as they are able to concentrate on what needs doing. Finally, managers who have been involved in benchmarking projects will, when asked, say that they 'know' their processes as opposed to those who have not, who are more inclined to say they 'think' they know.

## ENHANCED COMMUNICATION

Not only clarity of management but also the combination of activities involved in benchmarking, such as the debate and identification of what is important, the critical examination of how things are done and the discussions with people from outside the organization, develop a new range of 'opportunities to talk'. As new channels of communication open up, the opportunities for creativity and learning also increase. Consequently, the organization gradually becomes more proactive in its ability to assimilate and share new knowledge through the enhanced communication channels.

## ■ CHALLENGE CURRENT THINKING

Hewlett Packard is one company which regularly features on lists of potential partners and top performers across a range of process areas from product innovation to quality of working life. In 1994, Chairman Lew Platt was quoted[1] as saying 'Whatever we're doing that made us successful today won't be good in 1996, I can guarantee that. It might work in 1994. Maybe it'll even work in 1995, but it will kill you by 1996.'

It is precisely this kind of thinking which underpins the way successful benchmarking companies refuse to fall into the complacency trap. Managers are urged constantly to be looking out to the widest horizons of their environment in order to evaluate the next move. They know only too well that they are, in the words of Nissan UK Chief Executive,[2] either 'as good as the best or not good enough'. Challenging current thinking during benchmarking projects and encouraging people to step outside the immediate environment speeds up the amount of learning which is carried out in the organization, bringing new ideas and perspectives to bear on problems.

## ■ OPENS DOORS TO OTHER ORGANIZATIONS

Profitability, clarity of management and challenging current thinking are important benefits. However, the most significant reward referred to by operational benchmarkers is the way it provides a 'key' to open doors to organizations who would otherwise be inaccessible.

People feel more comfortable contacting a company they have never had dealings with before if they can base the discussion around the benefits of mutual learning from each other and their need for improvement. As long as the homework and preparation have been done thoroughly, the other party is more likely to be helpful than not. Furthermore, since benchmarking has become a household word there is little need for lengthy introduction to the topic – although it is always worth checking at the outset that both sides share the same interpretation of what is to be involved!

## EXTERNAL PERSPECTIVE

The external perspective which is gained from examining activities and processes through someone else's 'eyes', not least of all, the customers', proves invaluable. Much of the way we do what we do in the organization is conditioned by a combination of training, adaptation and culture. We rarely have the opportunity, time or reason to question this. Furthermore, if it works, why fix it?

However, asking customers how they perceive what you do or having someone from a different organization and culture ask what you do and why provides an ideal (and maybe long overdue) occasion to reconsider and evaluate your business.

## IMPROVED QUALITY OF WORKING LIFE

Being on the winning side, having clear leadership and management and transparent communications all add up to improved 'quality of working life'. Everybody works better for an organization that works well and is successful. However, people do not always recognize that they are excellent performers. Involvement in the improvement of processes enhances the way individuals value their contribution and that of their colleagues. This can lead to breaking down internal or sectional barriers (such as 'bought ledger' not talking to 'sales ledger' or 'marketing' not talking to 'development' sections).

Rank Xerox found that people working in 'best practice' processes do not recognize that they are doing things better than anyone else. It is simply 'the way they do things'. An outside facilitator is often required to tease out the factors which result in better performance. Thus, because nobody has taken the opportunity to look critically at what is going on or to establish whether there are better ways of doing everyday processes, mediocrity can often exist alongside excellence.

The 'outsider', who could be someone else in the organization who is benchmarking, or a representative from a 'visiting' or 'partnering' company, may have to work with the 'best practice' team to identify and draw out the reasons for their 'better' performance. Such extra attention raises the morale of the people engaged in the better process, making them feel special or more highly valued. Their self worth is enhanced and this in turn leads to a higher quality of working life.

Equally, those whose processes are improved as a result of this activity may benefit in similar measure.

## ■ INCREASED EFFICIENCY OF OPERATIONS

Productivity increases as quality improves because the amount of errors, rework and waste are reduced. Efficiencies transfer the previously wasted labour hours and machine time into the production of good product and better service. The resulting chain reaction is: 'lower costs, better competitive position, happier people on the job, jobs and more jobs'.[3]

One of the UK Post Office Counters Limited's earliest benchmarking activities identified a potential saving of almost one third of the overall cost of their cheque clearing process. This saving was directly attributable to removing operator errors and rework, which were identified when the team flow-charted the process. Such benefits clearly feed through to the bottom line.

HM Treasury similarly improved the process of opening the morning mail by reducing the number of people involved from three to one. In the original process, the first person 'opened' the envelope, the second person 'emptied' the envelope and separated incoming cheques from other types of content, and a third person checked there was nothing left in the envelope. Comparing this process with practices elsewhere led to a reduction in numbers with the other two operatives being deployed in other areas of the business.

The reader may think this story has been embellished, but it has not. It is not untypical of the 'stupidities' which creep into common practice. Nobody questions them because there has previously been no need to. The following is another example of what, with hindsight, was a ludicrous situation which existed for years before coming to light.

In the early days of privatization one of the major power utilities carried out an internal benchmarking project focusing on plant maintenance. Initial data collection and comparison identified that one of the smaller sites was consuming four times more water than any of the others, many of which were considerably larger. Site records showed the amount used to have been consistent over the years. The anomaly had not surfaced before because inter-site comparisons had not previously been made.

Analysis of the causes led to an astonishing revelation; a local farmer's supply had been linked in to the plant since the latter had been built – some 40 years previously. Stopping this 'leak' resulted in significant savings almost overnight.

Such simple examples illustrate how benchmarking feeds through to the bottom line. Analysis of processes helps identify non-value-adding elements, each of which taken in isolation may be relatively insignificant. Cumulatively, however, they have a considerable effect.

In the modern climate of lean efficient organizations and skill shortages, freeing up resources, which can then be deployed elsewhere, may be a more potent return than any straight financial gain.

Whichever is your prime objective, these and other benefits will only follow through if the common sense of the rigorous methodology outlined in Chapter 2 is coupled with a sound foundation on which to build, ensuring that the best becomes the only acceptable practice.

In the next chapter, therefore, we turn to some of the prerequisites for successful benchmarking.

## NOTES

1  *Financial Times,* 18 March 1994.
2  Quoted in an interview with BBC Radio 4 on 21.1.97 following the announcement of the Award to Nissan UK of £215 million investment won against Nissan Japan.
3  Deming, Edwards W. (1982) *Out of the Crisis,* Cambridge: Massachussetts Institute of Technology.

# CHAPTER

# 6

# READY FOR THE 'OFF'?

So far we have looked at what benchmarking is and where it came from, what the methodology involves and some of the benefits. But that does not mean that you are automatically going to get on and 'do' it.

Before you start you need to consider whether your organization is ready for benchmarking and whether it is the right 'tool' to use.

There are exceptions but most firms have found it useful to have an existing improvement culture. However, as we see later, this is not always practical or possible and certainly its absence should not be a deterrent to benchmarking. A typical continuum is shown in Figure 6.1 below.

Many organizations can trace the development of their improvement culture through the stages identified in this figure. Time and motion studies carried out in the 1960s led to statistical process control in the 1970s which, in turn, led to quality assurance. This developed into quality management during the late 1980s as firms recognized that this needed to be built in to the process rather than checked in at the end of it. In the UK, the British Standards[1] have evolved into International Standards[2] and many firms have progressed to Investors in People[3] recognition and, across Europe, self-assessment against the Business Excellence Model.

While it is easier to integrate benchmarking as part of continuing improvement initiatives, some firms have not enjoyed this luxury. Notable exceptions include companies formerly in the government sector which, as a direct result of privatization, moved rapidly into the 'quality first' century. Plunged virtually overnight into a competitive marketplace, many initiated benchmarking from the start to facilitate 'great leaps forward'. Many organizations carry out comparative or competitive analyses to establish where they are in relation to other firms in a given region or market. This is a natural precursor to benchmarking and can identify areas for improvement. Indeed, many people

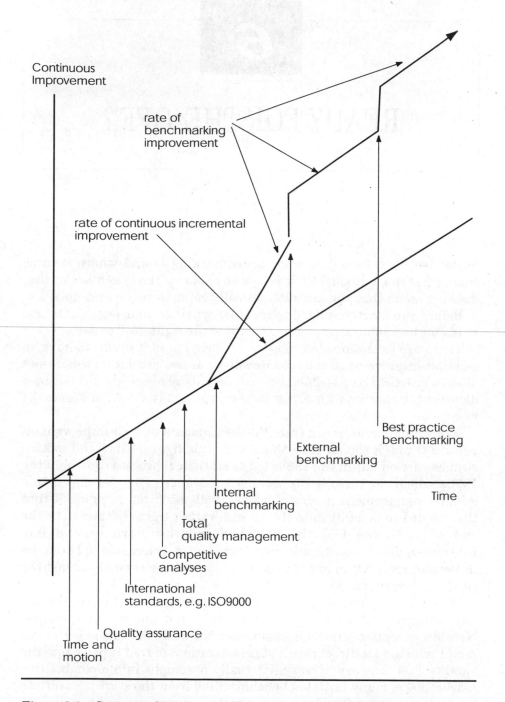

*Figure 6.1    Stages and initiatives along the improvement continuum*

believe that this *is* benchmarking. However, obtaining a picture of comparative standing within a defined peer group is not the same. The data gathered pinpoints:

○ areas of comparative strength, indicated by being positioned in the upper 'quartile' or section of the chart
○ areas of performance which equal those in the average 'median' quartile or middle section of the chart
○ areas of comparative weakness, indicated by a lower quartile, bottom of the chart, position.

The degree to which the results of such analyses provoke improvement or remedial activity will be determined by a series of factors, not least the objectives of the organization.

League tables provide a similar ranking or 'picture'. As indicated in Chapter 1 this can be extremely useful information. Many organizations regularly carry out this activity in order to keep abreast of the market. However, while it provides useful information, such analyses also raise many questions. The reports generated are based on current numeric data and are compiled with the aim of being extremely accurate. The organizations[4] who carry out this activity have to sanitize the data to keep it anonymous. If they did not do so, they could be accused by industry watchdogs of encouraging collusion or by participants of betraying confidential data. So, while providing information on how a firm compares with its peer group, the reports do not elaborate any details on who the better performers are, nor how they are achieving the better ranking. However, the comparative position may stimulate the need to introduce benchmarking.

Whether or not benchmarking is the right tool for the organization may also be determined by reviewing the prevailing culture. Factors which may provide an indication include:

○ How much importance is attached to needs of the customer (internal or external)?
○ How much pride is taken in the way work is done or services delivered?
○ What perception do 'outsiders' have of the company?
○ What is the prevailing atmosphere in the organization (are doors open or closed, for instance)?
○ Do people work in traditional offices or open plan environments?

These are among the considerations embodied in what has become known as the 'total quality management' (TQM) culture. Where this exists, benchmarking is often a logical 'next step' which ultimately becomes an integral component of the way things are done. TQM encourages everyone to focus on how well the internal and external customer is served in order to identify how much better they could be satisfied. Whereas this largely requires an inward focus, benchmarking enables the organization to scan the world outside its normal environment in order to discover excellent performers from whom new perspectives may be gained and lessons learned.

Sometimes the more successful the company appears to be, the less easy it is to gain commitment to improvement through a technique such as benchmarking. On the other hand, if there is a crisis looming, people may more readily be attracted to it.

In either situation, there must be a clear link between what the organization needs to achieve and how benchmarking is going to help. Unless this exists it will be very difficult to sustain commitment over the long term.

Furthermore, all benchmarking practitioners affirm that senior level commitment is the single most important factor for initiating projects and, subsequently, for the successful implementation of any project recommendations. This can only truly be given to an initiative which advances the organization's strategic intent. There must be a clear link between corporate objectives and benchmarking's role in realizing them. This must be recognized and interpreted at board level before the operational activities of benchmarking are instigated. The fundamental debate from which such a link should emerge addresses such questions as:

O   the business environment you are in
O   the basic principles and vision for the business
O   what the customers need
O   how the company is going to satisfy them
O   where the business ought to be in the future
O   how fast it needs to arrive there
O   what does this mean needs to be done in order to achieve that.

Discussion of such topics may lead to recognition that things are going to have to change, in which case benchmarking could be the ideal tool since it provides an organization with an excellent change facilitation process. But travelling this route necessitates some debate about the ramifications of altering the organization and whether it is ready to cope with and absorb the amount of disturbance that may result..

Figure 6.2, Table 6.1 and Figure 6.3 highlight questions to help focus attention in this area.

QUESTIONS CONCERNING READINESS TO ACCOMMODATE CHANGE

○ Is the pervading atmosphere one which accepts change as necessary and positive?
○ Is the operating environment one which is open to the world and new ideas?
○ Are individuals recognized and rewarded for taking the initiative?
○ Is genuine attention paid to customer needs?
○ Are suppliers viewed as partners?
○ Are employees encouraged to develop their skills and interests?
○ Are team working and multi-skilling encouraged?
○ Are the business leaders and managers approachable and ready to listen?
○ Are individuals open with, and helpful to, each other?

*Note:* Positive answers indicate greater readiness to change.

*Figure 6.2   Check list for a 'change' culture*

**Table 6.1   Traits which help and traits which hinder benchmarking**

| Traits which help benchmarking | Traits which hinder benchmarking | Critical trait |
| --- | --- | --- |
| Clear and cascaded goals | Goals not identified or 'fuzzy' | Yes |
| Flat, lean structure | Bureaucratic with many 'layers' | |
| Customer focus | Inward focus | Yes |
| Commitment to 'excellence' | Satisfied with status quo | Yes |
| Continuous improvement philosophy and activity | Quality assurance and checking | |
| Team approach to prevention and problem solving | Responsibility vested in single 'layer' or 'role' | Yes |
| Process management | People management | |
| Harmonious but challenging workstyle | Emphasis on rooting out failure rather than rewarding success | Yes |
| External focus | 'Not invented here' attitude prevails | |

| COSTS ASSOCIATED WITH INITIATING BENCHMARKING | REAL COST | OPPORTUNITY COST |
|---|---|---|
| Project management time | ✓ | ✓ |
| Training provision from outside for initial projects | ✓ | |
| Allocation for attendance at other learning events, e.g. conferences/seminars | ✓ | ✓ |
| Expert facilitation for early projects | ✓ | |
| Availability of team to do the work involved in the benchmarking initiatives | | ✓ |
| Expenses potentially incurred for visiting benchmarking partners | ✓ | |
| Cost of process mapping/re-engineering software and/or systems | ✓ | ✓ |
| Subscription to expert databases or centres of excellence | ✓ | |

*Figure 6.3*    *Costs associated with initiating benchmarking projects*

The use of consultants in the early stages of integrating benchmarking in the organization can be invaluable. They bring with them considerable experience of other industries and may help you avoid the frequently encountered pitfalls – like failing to plan activities carefully enough or being blinkered to other ways of doing things. They will think differently about the way in which your organization does or could function and their external perspective can, thus, prevent your team from being inward or industry focused.

Of course, consultants do not have to come from outside. Many organizations now have their own internal consultancy team or operation and this can be used very effectively. In addition, you should talk to people who are familiar with the ins and outs of the technique to learn from their experience of what is involved.

Having established the business need, and assured yourself that the right climate exists to sponsor learning, sharing and transferring best practices, make sure everyone involved understands what the objectives are and how benchmarking is going to bring benefits not only to the organization but to them as individuals.

Transparency of objectives and clarity of communication will help ensure that further down the line people do not get pulled away to do other things or fail to see benchmarking as important enough to spend time or effort on.

Having satisfied yourself that the foundations are in place and the organization is ready for the off you can now set out on the improvement journey. This is the focus of the next chapter.

## NOTES

1 The most common of which was BS5750 for quality of product.
2 BS5750 was replaced with ISO9000 and ISO9001.
3 An initiative driven by the UK Government through regional Training and Enterprise Councils to foster improved quality of product and working life by focusing on the development of the people in the enterprise.
4 Two organizations which specialize in this activity are PIMS (Profit Impact of Market Strategy) Associates Ltd who have operations across Europe and CIFC (Appendix 2: Centre for Interfirm Comparison) located in the UK. Details are provided in Appendix 2: Useful contacts.

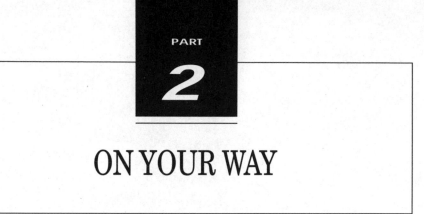

# ON YOUR WAY

# FULL STEAM AHEAD

The preceding chapters have explored the generality of what bench-marking is, the specifics of the methodology, the benefits that ensue and the things that ought to be considered before starting. In this chapter we make the assumption that someone in your organization has made the decision that benchmarking is the tool which is going to help the firm deliver its strategic objectives.

At this stage, the burden of responsibility shifts from the executive team and the board room (where strategic planning and decision-making usually reside) to the operational level. Maybe you are reading this book because someone has advised you that you now have responsibility for, or are about to become involved in, one of the company's benchmarking initiatives. They have probably added that they would like you to report back on your progress in three or six months' time.

The first task therefore is to produce the project plan. Continuous improvement is often described as a journey to 'world class' or 'excellence' and the concept of a journey is one which you should bear in mind as you compile your plan. You would hardly leave for a long holiday without considering where you were going (objectives), how you were going to get there (means and methods), who was going with you (the team) and what you needed to take along (skills and tools) to ensure everyone got the most out of their journey. You would probably also include a schedule of where you were going to be at various stages of your journey and when you expected to reach them (milestones).

Similarly your project plan should include:

○ a statement of objectives
○ the means and methods for achieving them
○ the team to be involved
○ the skills and tools they need
○ the extent of the budget to be set aside and how it will be deployed

○    how much time will be required
○    what will be the major milestones and
○    when you expect to be able to see results
○    when, how and to whom to report

Although this may sound time consuming the essence of successful benchmarking lies in tight project planning from the beginning. You should provide all team members with a copy of the plan so that:

○    they can keep the overall picture in mind while completing their individual tasks
○    they know which responsibilities other team members are carrying out at any point and the impact of their own contribution, particularly if this is delayed and impairs the progress of the project at any stage
○    they can use it to help colleagues understand the project and the extent of their involvement in it.

The growing recognition of the importance of project management across the range of business operations is leading to the introduction in the market of an increasing number of software tools.[1] These are invaluable in coordinating the numerous strands of a complex project's activities.

Once the project plan has been drawn up you are ready to involve the key players (Figure 7.1). This should be as small a group as possible, while recognizing the variety of activities which need to be involved.

---

| | |
|---|---|
| *Executive champion* | Representing senior level commitment to ensure that benchmarking is coordinated with strategy and integrated with other major change initiatives; responsibilities include keeping leaders fully briefed on strategic issues which impinge on the project, mentoring the leader on his presentation of recommendations for other members of the senior team so that they are universally debated and accepted as appropriate, greasing the political wheels where and as appropriate; acting as back-up if the leader requires extra force behind the arrangement of site visits |
| *Leader* | Initially chosen by the executive champion but later elected by the team(s). This person could be the owner of the specific process being |

*Figure 7.1    Players in the benchmarking team*

benchmarked. His responsibilities involve accepting the brief from the champion, ensuring that he understands the brief, briefing others on the team, liaising with the facilitator to ensure objectives of the project are met; liaising with the project coordinator to ensure that milestones and targets are agreed, determining what level of information needs to be communicated across the organization and towards the public

*Project coordinator*    Could be the leader but is responsible for 'running the project' – being briefed by the leader, agreeing deadlines and milestones, ensuring team players are kept involved where appropriate and briefed, convening meetings, arranging site visits, coordinating all deadlines and communicating with others outside the team: coopting the various team players as and when they are needed but priming them in advance, providing backup to the leader where it is required, e.g. for senior level presentation material or outside presentation to partners

*Facilitator*    Chosen by the leader for the life-time of the project team. Facilitates all teams meetings and discussions as well as being present at the site visits; must liaise fully before each meeting with the leader and/or project coordinator to ensure objectives are clear and debrief afterwards to agree if they have been met; responsible for ensuring that all meeting time is fully utilized; for observing group skills and behaviour and making recommendations to the project coordinator where and if further team players are needed. May work on more than one benchmarking project at a time

*Team player*    At different times in the project, different people may be needed on the team; members will need to bring key skills with them – such as analytical skills, work process documentation skills, information search and analysis skills, if appropriate a customer of or supplier to the process. Team players should be fully briefed by the team leader on their role and level of contribution and should agree to give that their commitment. Must be made fully responsible for ensuring they know what is going on and asking questions if at any time they are unsure of their roles and tasks

*Figure 7.1    Players in the benchmarking team (concluded)*

| Team role | Key skills required | Level of benchmarking expertise |
|---|---|---|
| Executive champion | Leadership, communication | Executive overview fit with strategy |
| Project leader | Leadership, team building, communication, presentation | Overview and awareness of practicalities |
| Project coordinator | Project management, presentation | Theory and practice of methodology |
| Facilitator | Facilitation, communications | Theory and practice of methodology |
| Team player | According to input: process analysis, documentation, data scanning, information search, etc. | Overview of the methodology and fit of particular skills mix |
| Customer/supplier | External perspective on the process; objectivity; communication | Executive overview unless involved in process analysis when more detail of its role required |

*Figure 7.2   Benchmarking team mix and skills required*

Since the subject area for the benchmarking has already been selected you have an idea of who to involve. Your choice of team members should be based on a combination of their role in that area and their match of skills against tasks which need to be performed (Figure 7.2).

You must also consider their availability and willingness to be included. They should have sufficient time to be actively involved and be willing to spend that time freely. If you need people from other areas, functions or departments, their direct manager should be prepared to release them for the time required for team activities. Table 7.1 below indicates the amount of their working time that team members will need to allocate to the benchmarking project. However, it should also be borne in mind that one result of benchmarking any process is that it will be 'cleaned up' or simplified and will, therefore, take less time on every subsequent occasion it is performed. Ultimately, therefore, the initial time investment will be repaid many times.

| TABLE 7.1 Allocation of time required from team members for benchmarking projects (percentages are a proportion of total working time) | | | | |
|---|---|---|---|---|
| Role | Time | Time | Time | Time |
| | 1–10% | 1-25% | 1–50% | 50–100% |
| Executive champion | ✓ | | | |
| Leader | | | ✓ | |
| Project coordinator | | | | ✓ |
| Facilitator | | | ✓ | |
| Various team players | | ✓ | | |
| Customer of/ supplier to process | ✓ | | | |

If any of your initial selection of members does not fit the team criteria they will be ineffective and are thus best left out. Your focus in early projects is to ensure objectives are met and that sponsors are convinced of the benefits and value of benchmarking. Picking team members who will later cause difficulties or have to drop out or be replaced is an avoidable pitfall.

Team members will encounter stress and become demotivated if it seems that some participants are giving more time and shouldering more of the work than others. Yet it is unreasonable to expect everyone to do exactly the same amount. A useful team-building tool is the 'commitment' contract which can be drawn up at the beginning of team activities. This enables everyone to say honestly, without fear of recrimination, how much time they believe they can realistically devote to the team's activities. This could vary from an hour a week to several hours a day. Its strengths lie in:

○ forcing everyone to face the reality of their time constraints
○ discussing these and
○ thereby making a genuine and considered commitment.

This procedure enables all team members to become aware of each other's contribution. When signed, the contract serves as a useful reminder that even though each person's time on project activities may vary, the level of commitment is equal.

An example of such a contract used within an engineering firm is provided in Figure 7.3. The document sets out very clearly what the objectives, mission and key requirements of the project are and team members have then signed and dated the appropriate section, writing alongside how much time each was prepared to allocate. Copies were then provided to all the team players to keep with their documentation and serve as a reminder.

---

BENCHMARKING – 'PERSONNEL ON-COSTS'

OBJECTIVES/MISSION

To investigate and identify opportunities to significantly reduce costs in the abovementioned areas by carrying out a bench-marking process to identify:

a)   target levels for key metrics
b)   process improvements to support achievement of the targets

and, finally, to report recommendations for change to the Board.

*Key requirements:*

1.   to understand the benchmarking process
2.   to develop short and long-term strategies to achieve objectives
3.   to produce a plant of action to identify and implement early improvements
4.   to plan for longer term permanent reduction in all these areas of waste by benchmarking best practice companies.

*Mission statement:*

To investigate and identify opportunities to significantly reduce costs in the abovementioned areas by carrying out a benchmarking process to identify:

a)   target levels for key metrics
b)   process improvements to support achievements of the targets

and, finally, to report recommendations for change to the Board.

*Figure 7.3    Example of a benchmarking team commitment contract*

*Boundaries of project:*

None identified at this stage.

*Resources:*

A BP Team has been set up to investigate the symptoms, the underlying processes and to gather appropriate data and analyse this to enable improvement recommendations to be made. The team is receiving appropriate project based training as the project unfolds.

The level of commitment required for each team member is expected to be eight hours per week.

| Team member's name | Approved team member signature | Date | Hours commitment |
|---|---|---|---|
| J. SMITH | *J. Smith* | 10.9.96 | 8 hrs |
| P. COOK | *P. Cook* | — | 16 hrs |
| R. JAMES | *R. James* | — | 4 hrs |
| F. HARROD | *F. Harrod* | 13.9.96 | 1 hr |
| P. SHAW | *P. Shaw* | — | 6 hrs |
| E. CLARKE | *E. Clarke* | — | 4 hrs |
| M. ODER | *M. Oder* | 10.9.96 | 4 hrs |
| Leader: | *J. P. Jomnes* | 15.9.96 | 8 hrs |
| Facilitator. | *O. D. Fell* | 10.9.96 | 8 hrs |
| Project sponsor: | *W. Eccles* | 16.9.96 | 1 hr |

*Figure 7.3   Example of a benchmarking team commitment contract (concluded)*

Team briefings are the fuel which drives the project along its journey. The first of these should cover all aspects of the project plan and include consideration of the training required. Table 7.2 provides a synopsis of the training which may be required at different points in the project.

| Table 7.2 | Just in time training for the benchmarking team | |
| --- | --- | --- |
| *When* | *Who* | *What* |
| Before the project | Executive | Overview, strategy and resource consideration |
| At kick off | Project coordinator and team leader | Practical workshop on methodology, resource and project management + focus on process analysis |
| After selection of process | Team players | Practical benchmarking and syndicate work on own process |
| Before approaching outside partners | Team players | Data sources and collection for identifying partners |
| Before approaching partners | Team players involved at this stage | Protocol and procedure questionnaire and preparation to optimize exchange |
| During data gathering and comparison | Team players conducting analysis of performance differences | Quality tools workshop for discerning and displaying process performance and improvement |
| Before implementation | Project coordinator and project leaders | Min. one day workshop on communication and implementation planning |
| During implementation | Project leader | Regular monitoring and review sessions against milestones |

Whether you develop your own training using the methodology out-lined in Chapter 2, or call in outside experts,[2] the important factor is to ensure that all those involved in the project 'speak the same language'. So, if you use outside training courses, use the same provider. If you develop in-house courses, make sure everyone in the organization is aware of them. One of the most effective ways of ensuring that a common language and terminology develops is to take advantage of distance learning products. These are available as computer-based training packages, CD-ROM suites, video and audio cassettes and enable individuals to access whichever learning mode suits them or their time constraints best.[3]

The next most important task insofar as getting started is concerned is to open up the communications process with the rest of the organization. In Chapter 2 we saw that communication is Step 9 in the formal methodology. This is because without it, implementation of benchmarking recommendations stands little chance of success. However, the best way to ensure an easy passage from the analytical to the practical aspects of the project is to start rolling out the communication plan alongside the project plan.

Some firms accomplish this by including regular benchmarking updates in their corporate newsletters, others by having a series of briefings or simply posting regular communications about what is happening on wall and intranet noticeboards. The best communication processes are proactive and two-way, so that the good ideas which exist around the organization are encouraged and contributed. The situation where benchmarking findings are suddenly 'sprung' on the organization is not uncommon but should be avoided at all costs.

The journey is now well advanced. To recapitulate progress so far, you have:

O    drawn up the project plan
O    involved and, where appropriate, trained the team
O    initiated the process of communication across the organization.

The route is now determined by the process as you begin 'peeling back the onion'. Following the steps described in Chapter 2 leads to uncovering where the problems or the opportunities for improvement exist. In this way an initial focus on the 'supply chain' may highlight the need to monitor supplier's product quality. This could lead in turn to realization of the fact that data which is required about such quality is either very scant or spread across disparate parts of the organization and, thus, difficult to gather. Benchmarking may actually be carried out, therefore, on the internal process for collecting accurate data on supplier quality. Subsequent projects may focus on the monitoring and improving of their performance.

As the above example illustrates, it may be necessary to peel back several layers of the onion. The closer you can focus the area of the process you need to improve the easier it will be to brainstorm for partners. It is important that you do not try to cover everything in one project – you will be en route too long and the organizational span of attention may not be sufficient. Instead, segment your journey into manageable chunks, progressing through the methodology as set out in Chapter 2. When completed, let the organization know that you have arrived successfully at your goal. That way, you will secure greater enthusiasm for the next journey.

Full steam ahead may sound straightforward. However, benchmarking is a repetitive process and you should be prepared to circle occasionally or seemingly go backwards before moving ahead. This is normal and far better than falling into the trap of sacrificing success to 'completion at all costs'.

As projects deliver successful outcomes and benchmarking becomes a recognized way of initiating improvement, attention will shift to the considerations of managing and resourcing a number of concurrent benchmarking activities.

This is the subject of the next chapter.

## NOTES

1   Using a project management software package can be invaluable for ensuring that activities are fully coordinated. As with all software tools, however, you should seek advice from users as well as product specialists, and test out the packages, before making up your mind which is best for you.
2   The Benchmarking Centre Limited based in Gerrards Cross, Buckinghamshire, UK, can provide training across the spectrum of needs.
3   *The Case for Benchmarking* published by Oak MultiMedia Ltd incorporates the complete range of project tools in a variety of media. (See Appendix 2: Useful contacts.)

CHAPTER

*8*

# RESOURCES FOR THE CONTINUING JOURNEY

Assuming that initial projects have been successful and enthusiasm for, and commitment to, benchmarking in the organization are now assured, consideration should be given to the longer term management and resource implications. Relevant frameworks need to be developed to enable benchmarking to be integrated into the 'everyday' culture. A single project can be managed fairly easily (although that may not be the perception at the time); two or three projects can be managed by the same person if they are doing virtually nothing else; but the number of projects will escalate and with them the amount of time required of a coordinator. In this chapter, therefore, we shift our focus: from 'managing for initial success' to 'managing for long-term success'.

Planning ahead will help in avoiding three of the most frequent pitfalls which are:

1.  more than one team from different parts of your organization visiting the same people at another one and not knowing it. This is frustrating for both sides and gives a very unprofessional impression which is hardly a basis for long-term partnerships
2.  different parts of the organization benchmarking the same process without knowing it. This obviously duplicates effort and resource required, but a greater danger is that it signals inability to transfer learning
3.  groups or individuals benchmarking without clear direction, co-ordination or knowledge that others internally are engaged in similar activities.

This sort of activity may lead to improvement but many wheels are reinvented along the way and it takes much longer to build up the critical mass of energy which results in long-term benefit.

There are three modes of operating which avoid these eventualities, although they are effectively extensions of each other:

1.  *the central coordinator* – based on an individual
2.  *the corporate best practice hub* – based on an office, which could be real or virtual
3.  *the best practice repository* – based on a databank.

Each is considered in turn below.

## ■ THE CENTRAL COORDINATOR

As the title suggests, one person is assigned the role of coordinating and recording all the benchmarking activity within the enterprise. All outward bound contacts and incoming requests (from others wishing to benchmark against the organization) go through the same person. The coordinator's responsibilities are:

1.  to ensure that the various benchmarking projects within the company are conducted openly and ethically
2.  to advise and liaise with project team leaders regarding their requirements – hardware, software, skills training, people, time – and, as far as reasonably possible, to ensure these are made available at optimum time and cost
3.  to coordinate all benchmarking projects so that resources are used efficiently, thus avoiding unnecessary duplication or overlapping
4.  to agree the level and frequency of data and documentation that should be recorded and shared between the different benchmarking teams and organize regular information sharing events for them
5.  to act as the public relations advisor and liaison between benchmarking projects/activities and the rest of the organization to 'grease the wheels' and to minimize the risk of surprises
6.  accordingly to mastermind the communication and information flows with regard to the benchmarking activities
7.  to maintain a perspective which is wider than the immediate process improvement in order to ensure that the overall objectives of the organization are kept in the frame
8.  to ensure no rogue projects (i.e. those which do not align with organizational objectives) are going on
9.  to prioritize the number of projects conducted at any time so the overall direction and impact of improvement activity is not diluted.

The coordinator has a high profile which requires considerable liaison with the top team.

# THE CORPORATE BEST PRACTICE HUB

In a small organization, it is reasonable to expect one person to coordinate all benchmarking activities. In larger or multi-site enterprises, however, the coordination may be conducted via a 'benchmarking' or 'best practice' office which serves as the global hub for all such activity. This hub could be located in the headquarters or main production site with individual coordinators appointed at each operating unit across the range of countries in which the company is active. Alternatively, it could be located at a particular site on the corporate intranet in to which individuals at the various locations may feed data and information.

The central hub is staffed by a corporate coordinator, support administrator and best practice facilitators. The latter need not necessarily be full time in this role but may be called in to teams as the need arises. In addition to the responsibilities of the coordinator in the first model, the role of the hub extends to:

1. selecting the right people as 'satellite' coordinators and ensuring they are fully briefed and trained to carry out their responsibilities
2. devolving responsibility for the day-to-day benchmarking activity to the site coordinators, while maintaining an overview of activities
3. holding regular briefing meetings between the hub and satellite coordinators to share experiences with, and learn from, each other
4. selecting and, where necessary, training facilitators and in-house experts who can be 'used' across the different sites to identify the improvement opportunities and to ensure continuity of language, policy and practice as well as transfer of learning
5. developing mechanisms to locate if and where best practices exist in the organization
6. bringing these to the attention of the locations who are in need of, or searching for, best practices
7. maintaining links and networks with other organizations to ensure that the internal best practices are comparable with, or can be enhanced by, external best practices.

## THE BEST PRACTICE REPOSITORY

Effectively the basic requirements are an accessible and idiot proof networked databank system and someone to act as 'bank manager'. This could be the central coordinator described in (1) above or the best practice unit described in (2) and is dependent on the size of the organization.

The system provides a database of all the established benchmarks, gathered from internal and external activities as well as a complete log of all benchmarking projects in the organization under key headings such as those suggested in Table 8.1.

As processes are benchmarked, the data and information from the activity are logged into the databank by a designated person. This could be someone on an individual project or a person centrally responsible for all project data. All process maps and linked data should be available to everyone in the organization, although access for making changes is best restricted to a few known databank managers.

When further improvement activity results in the development of better practices or more efficient and effective processes, the relevant data/information is logged in centrally and overwrites that previously contained on the computer. Anyone tapping in to the databank can thereby have access to current best practice. This maintains 'process vitality' and avoids units around the organization reinventing the wheel each time a process is benchmarked.

Two factors are essential to ensure that the system is effective:

1.  it must be regularly monitored and kept up-to-date with sound, reliable information and
2.  it must be readily available and easily accessible to everyone in the organization otherwise it will not be consulted in the course of improvement projects.

Failing either of the above a situation will develop where the databank is not consulted and as a result previous activities, learning or development of best practices are not factored in to current projects. Duplications will occur or mistakes recur; results are not logged and improvements not communicated. Eventually the whole system breaks down.

| Table 8.1 | Items for inclusion in a benchmarking databank |
| --- | --- |

| What | Why |
| --- | --- |
| Project title | To identify where the project stems from and what it is about |
| Project ID | A code number/letter which can be used as a short form of the title |
| Process focused on | Prevents duplication, ensures updates are coordinated |
| Project time | Identifies whether past or present and duration |
| Project leader | Identifies who to talk to to obtain detailed/anecdotal information |
| Contact details | Where, when and how to get hold of the person – increasingly they will not necessarily be in the same location |
| Benchmarking partner organization and why selected | May spark off some other thoughts in other project teams |
| Brief outline of the partner organization | Saves time on the part of the team accessing the database |
| Contact name and details | Provides others who may wish to access same organization with starting point |
| Any other key information such as whether the organization was part of another holding company, or later acquired, etc. | Provides a rapid starting ramp for the next team if they are still interested in contacting the same organization; internal sharing of information |

## DEALING WITH INBOUND REQUESTS TO PARTNER OTHERS

Once your internal affairs have been resolved you will need to spend some time thinking about the external ramifications of striving continuously to be the best. Before long, companies looking for partners to benchmark against will start adding your name to their list. Perhaps they have done so already and you are finding yourself inundated with numerous requests from potential partners!

A likely first reaction is to feel flattered and, if it is coupled with a genuine desire to help others up the improvement curve, that may continue for a while. However, there will come a point when someone says, 'Hey, we should focus on the business rather than helping others – otherwise we'll be out of business ourselves!'

In other words, you could find your company in the position of being so helpful to others that your employees take their eyes off the ball and gradually your performance record starts to slip.

A number of long-term benchmarking companies such as IBM, Xerox and Hewlett Packard have learned to shoulder the burden of helping others without damage to their core business. They have set up specific systems to cope with incoming requests. In most cases these involve rigorous screening – one organization is cited as having a 17-page questionnaire for potential visitors to complete – or restricted access on a few selected dates in the year.

Your organization will face, and have to resolve, the same dilemmas. The central coordinator should be able to handle all the issues, but only if it is clearly communicated inside and outside the organization that s/he is the person responsible for all contact and liaison on improvement projects.

Long-term success of best practice improvement activity will result if projects are efficiently coordinated and managed. Communications channels need to be kept well oiled so that everyone knows who is the responsible first point of contact for all activity.

However, there are a number of other factors which have proved to contribute to the success of benchmarking in terms of benefit to the organization. These are elaborated in the next chapter.

# CHAPTER

# *9*

---

# THE KEY SUCCESS FACTORS

---

The previous chapter explored the long-term management issues surrounding the import, sharing and transfer of best practices across the organization and ended on the suggestion that success would follow from effective communication and coordination. This chapter sets out other notable success factors which have been identified by seasoned benchmarkers (Figure 9.1).

---

KEY SUCCESS FACTORS FOR BENCHMARKING

Commitment and leadership from the top of the organization

Internal commitment supported by externally visible commitment

Common language and methodology across the organization

Self-assessment against recognized framework

Focus on competencies

Speedily disseminate and transfer learning and best practices

Teach people to fish

Choose effective implementers

---

*Figure 9.1    Key success factors for benchmarking projects*

## ◼ LEADERSHIP AND COMMITMENT FROM THE TOP

The prime factor in the success of all benchmarking projects is genuine leadership and commitment from the most senior level in the organization. Key individuals responsible for seeing benchmarking projects through must not be hauled off to resolve a crisis, given other priorities by their direct managers or simply swamped with increasing amounts of work and responsibility at the same time as trying to launch initial benchmarking projects. Furthermore, if the project leader leaves the organization somebody else must pick up the reins; otherwise, activity simply ceases and in all likelihood the project will fail.

It is essential that strong commitment and leadership are visible from the top of the organization. The senior executive officers must comprehend both the concept and the theory of benchmarking. Together they must identify whether and how the technique can help the organization achieve its 'strategic' objectives or intent. In addition, the resource commitment – budget, people, and time – must be recognized and built in to the business plan in order to ensure that the individuals involved are able to deliver on the projects.

Responsibility for delivering improvement should be built in to the objectives at each managerial level and, ultimately, the annual assessment and development plans of all individuals.

## ◼ INTERNAL COMMITMENT SUPPORTED BY EXTERNALLY VISIBLE COMMITMENT

Successful benchmarking results through effective networking across the broadest boundaries. Commitment to continuous improvement should be visible internally and externally. The objective of networking is to access and learn about best practices and to find partners. One of the easiest ways to find suitable ones is to have them come to you. This may well happen via the grapevine, but will be much more likely if you broadcast your improvement activities, successes or needs in order that others hear about them and seek you out. Hence, corporate communications, annual reports and other publicity and marketing material should all include relevant references.

## ◼ COMMON LANGUAGE AND METHODOLOGY

As with all long-term programmes, there must be a common language and 'way of doing benchmarking' across the entire organization at every location. This will need support and reinforcement through communication, training and awareness sessions. If the situation arises where everyone is able to 'do benchmarking' in any way they please, activity will be haphazard and lead to only patchy benefit. The co-ordinating mechanisms outlined in the previous chapter are the means whereby the language and method are shared.

## ◼ SELF-ASSESSMENT

Self-assessment is essential to the success of benchmarking. Unless you know where you are and how you are performing today, how will you know where you are going or recognize if you have got anywhere? Recognized frameworks such as the Business Excellence Model described in Chapter 2 provide a means whereby companies can establish their current position and use this as a marker against which to set improvement goals. Regular annual assessment against the same criteria enable long term trends and comparisons to be made.

In this way companies can talk about their success with the benefit of hindsight. It is also why completed case studies – with benefits and outcomes fully documented – take considerable time to develop. It is often not until the knock-on effects of cumulative benchmarking projects have become visible that companies begin to recognize the true value of each individual exercise. Figure 9.2 identifies typical maturity and pay-back periods.

##  FOCUS ON COMPETENCIES

Successful outcomes depend on focusing improvement projects with laser sharpness on areas most likely to result in the greatest advantage. This avoids the 'headless chicken' syndrome where everybody rushes round blindly trying to improve everything with little, if any, thought to overall business objectives and strategy. The core competen-

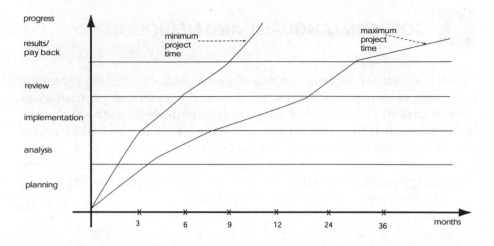

*Figure 9.2    Typical minimum and maximum results / pay-back periods for benchmarking projects*

cies approach described in Chapter 2 is arguably the most effective way of developing sharp focus. Furthermore, it ensures that a longer term, top-down, total business perspective is taken.

## SPEEDILY DISSEMINATE AND TRANSFER LEARNING AND BEST PRACTICES

In dynamic markets survival may depend on the speed at which new learning and thinking is spread internally throughout an organization. Hence, the infrastructure must be developed to enable individuals to learn, share and develop best practices increasingly effectively and quickly. Development of frameworks such as the models for communication and control, identified in Chapter 8, are essential to success. Unless the lessons and successes from benchmarking are disseminated by such means the impetus for further projects will be difficult to sustain in the face of other business exigencies.

## TEACH PEOPLE TO 'FISH'

There is a saying that 'if you give a man a fish, you feed him for a day, but if you teach him to fish, you feed him for life'. Likewise with benchmarking. Although, in theory, you can get third party organizations to come in and supply the service of 'doing the benchmarking for you' (feeding you fish), long-term benefits and success can only be secured through teaching your own people to benchmark (fish) for themselves. Even if you hire consultants, your team are going to have to 'do' the work which results from the reports and recommendations. The most effective way of ensuring successful follow through on projects, therefore, is to give 'internal' people the tools and training to do the planning and analysis themselves, so that they 'own' the action plans which result. By all means, use outside experts to help develop your in-house material but rapidly transfer the knowledge across to your own personnel.

## ■ CHOOSE EFFECTIVE IMPLEMENTERS

Benchmarking is a phased activity involving different skills at the various stages. The team needs planners in the first stage and analysers in the second. However, if implementers are not selected, preferably well in advance of the third stage, the organization is in danger of getting elegant benchmarking studies but no resultant improvement benefit.

Implementers can be recognized by their energy and action orientation and are rarely the same people who carry out good planning or analysis. Quite often they are mavericks; they 'get things done' by speaking up, bending the rules, cajoling and politicking or whatever other means they need to achieve their objectives. If benchmarking projects – particularly early ones – are to succeed, the top team (or the project leader) must identify the implementers early on and ensure they are appropriately prepared for their involvement.

Frankly, none of the success factors covered above will be of help unless you make the first step forward. So often, people gather information about benchmarking to gauge whether it is the 'right tool' and will work for them. They prove to their satisfaction that this is the case. Nothing further happens. Or, worse still, they fear committing themselves to getting started, so they carry on collecting increasing amounts of information as if to build up a safety barrage between themselves and the eventual improvement project.

It is rather like riding a bike – once you have been taught the basic techniques, the only way you are going to find out if it works and what makes for success is to get on and have a go! Progress may be a bit wobbly to start with and you may even 'fall off' a couple of times, but gradually everything will come together and you will wonder what all the fuss was about.

In order to reinforce this point, the next chapter provides an excellent example of how one organization in the public sector conducted an initial benchmarking project on a process in the human resources area.

# CASE STUDY

CHAPTER

*10*

# THE THEORY IN PRACTICE: VACANCY FILLING IN THE EMPLOYMENT SERVICES

Readers of books on management techniques and theory are inclined to think: 'OK, that's how you're supposed to do it but surely nobody actually follows the theory so rigorously'. That may well be true in any number of cases. Repeatedly, however, it has been proved in benchmarking that despite the concepts being so simple, success only follows from rigorous application of the methodology.

The following case study provides an excellent example for anyone new to benchmarking. It was the winning submission in 1997 of the European Best Practice Benchmarking Award™[1] and illustrates succinctly how the organization achieved a successful outcome from the project.

The Employment Service had identified a problem in its recruitment process with particular regard to the amount of time taken to fill vacancies. The case study documents the reasons why it was decided to resolve the problem using benchmarking techniques, what was involved throughout and the results achieved. Although the technique had been used in the Employment Service before, this was the first occasion on which it has been applied in the human resources context.

## NOTE

1   Awarded annually by The Benchmarking Centre Ltd in the UK to organizations across Europe whose benchmarking project case study submissions are considered exemplars of best practice in the technique. Among other criteria, the judges look for evidence of clear planning, analysis and implementation with proven results following through from process improvements. Previous winners have included Hewlett Packard Finance and Remarketing Division, IBM Call Management Centre, Shell Exploration

and Production, and HM Customs and Excise. The runner up to Employment Services in 1997 was BT. Full details of the Award are available from The Benchmarking Centre Limited, Gerrards Cross, UK.

*Winner*

THE EUROPEAN BEST PRACTICE

BENCHMARKING AWARD™
1997

**Business Category**

EUROPEAN BEST PRACTICE
BENCHMARKING AWARD 1997

BUSINESS CATEGORY

THE EMPLOYMENT SERVICE
BENCHMARKING STUDY:
INTERNAL FILLING

'RADICALLY REDUCING THE ELAPSED
TIME FOR FILLING VACANCIES'

# INTRODUCTION

1.1    The Employment Service (ES) is a large government agency within the Department for Education and Employment [DfEE]. It is responsible for: helping jobseekers, particularly those that have been out of work six months or more, to find work or a placement on an employment or training programme; and ensuring that jobseekers who claim Job Seekers Allowance (JSA) are entitled to receive it. It delivers these services through a District Structure consisting of a national network of some 1 200 ES Jobcentres (ESJs). These districts are supported by nine Regional Offices and Head Office. The ES employs approximately 35 000 people, most of whom are based in ESJs.

1.2    This case study describes the ES approach to the use of benchmarking as a tool by looking at how it was used to improve a key human resource process – internal vacancy filling. It covers:

O    *leadership*: why we decided to use benchmarking and sponsorship of the project
O    *process*: how we went about benchmarking vacancy filling
O    *results*: how we have developed proposals as a result of the study and implemented improvements to the vacancy filling system.

# LEADERSHIP

## BENCHMARKING IN ES

2.1    The ES has made a public commitment to continuous improvement and has encouraged managers at every level in the organization to review working practices to improve performance. As part of this commitment ES has systematically set about reviewing and improving its processes. The first stage in this was high level mapping of all ES key processes using IDEF/O.*

2.2    This commitment to improving its processes through a systematic use of process improvement tools is in response to the need to:

O    improve the quality of service to customers in a rapidly changing labour market

---

* **CAM DEF**inition method (where ICAM is Integrated Computer Aided Manufacturing) was developed by the US Dept of Defence in the 1970s and is used to describe processes. It uses a tap down method which goes from the general to the specific, from a single page (Level 0) to more detailed pages explaining how subsections of the system work.

○    increase efficiency so as to operate effectively within reduced resources
○    deliver against Government initiatives to encourage greater efficiency within Government departments and agencies; these were set out in the White Paper 'Continuity and Change'.

2.3    To promote this commitment, ES has run a number of seminars and workshops for its managers. The most notable of these was a series entitled 'Continuity and Change' where managers were asked to consider various process improvement techniques, e.g. business process analysis, market testing, benchmarking, etc., to identify the benefits they could bring to the management of their processes. These seminars also set benchmarking in the context of wider change management in the organization. ES communicated the outcomes from these seminars to the rest of the organization through its internal newsletter 'Inside ES'.

2.4    As a result, benchmarking is considered within ES as a very important improvement tool, but only one among many. Its use and effectiveness is therefore reviewed along with other initiatives through senior forums, chief executive people reviews and feedback mechanisms.

2.5    Benchmarking has been used in ES to:

○    compare functional activities to answer the question? 'How well are we doing?'
○    underpin fundamental process reviews to identify better practices to draw into the wider project
○    internally to identify areas of difference.

2.6    This project attempted to draw on all three approaches and was the first time process benchmarking had been applied in a systematic way to improve a major HR (human resources) process.

## WHY DID WE DECIDE TO USE BENCHMARKING TO IMPROVE THE INTERNAL VACANCY FILLING SYSTEM ?

2.7    The ES introduced a competence based vacancy filling system in 1994 for people in its management pay bands (MPBs), approximately one-third of its workforce is covered by these arrangements. Since its inception the system has been the subject of criticism and debate, mainly because it is perceived by customers/users as time consuming and resource intensive.

2.8    A major external review of the system, which involved all key stakeholders, identified a number of strengths (these were significant enough for ES to decide it wanted to keep the system) and a number of weaknesses. Customer feedback from the evaluation, regular monitoring of the system and a large consultation exercise supported these findings. The Director of HR therefore decided that we needed to improve the process to increase customer confidence in the system and to reduce the amount of time and resources used.

2.9 Therefore prior to the start of our study we had the added advantage that customers and senior managers wanted to see change. In fact the status quo was something we could no longer consider.

2.10 Benchmarking was chosen as the preferred improvement tool following a meeting of key stakeholders which discussed how best to address the weaknesses. It was chosen because it would give us a better understanding of the vacancy filling process (including times and costs) and it was hoped that it would help us identify 'break through' improvements, which had not been forthcoming from other avenues we had explored, through a systematic comparison of our system with the best in other organizations.

## HOW IS BENCHMARKING SPONSORED IN ES?

2.11 To encourage the use of benchmarking in ES a benchmarking management group consisting of senior managers from head office and the regions was set up to oversee benchmarking projects. This was supported at a working level by management consultants in an ES head office division – Process and Systems Division – who were responsible for disseminating information on benchmarking to the rest of the organization and acting as a 'Gateway' for benchmarking, i.e. they help people set up benchmarking projects and support those projects if needed.

2.12 Training has mainly, with the exception of those directly involved in the projects, been limited to awareness raising particularly among senior and middle managers through presentations and seminars conducted by internal consultants and external experts.

2.13 ES still considers itself on a learning curve with regard to the use of benchmarking and it was therefore important that we drew out any learning about its use from this study. However, we did follow a defined and well-documented model for our benchmarking activities based on the one encouraged by The Benchmarking Centre to which ES is a member (appendix 1).

2.14 The vacancy filling study was sponsored by the Director of Human Resources (HR). He took an active interest in the study and the use of benchmarking throughout the project, keeping himself abreast of developments through interim reports and Keep In Touch (KIT) meetings.

2.15   To support our benchmarking initiatives and external relations, ES plays an active part in a number of fora that promote benchmarking as a performance improvement tool – most notably through membership of The Benchmarking Centre and attendance at the Civil Service Benchmarking Networking Group. These all provided an invaluable source of information during our study into vacancy filling.

2.16   Members of the division who are responsible for supporting the ES benchmarking effort, and members of the team responsible for undertaking the benchmarking study into vacancy filling, have received comprehensive training in the use of benchmarking and analytical techniques. The training for the latter group was provided by Coopers and Lybrand. In addition, senior managers and key stakeholders have received either awareness training or in-depth briefing on benchmarking.

2.17   To date benchmarking in ES can be described as having the following features:

O   a faculty centre which is based in the Process and Systems Division which acts as a 'gateway' for those interested in undertaking a benchmarking study and is the knowledge base
O   local sponsorship of projects based on ownership of the process, but at a very senior level
O   a systematic review of processes.

2.18   These features all applied in the vacancy filling study.


## PROCESS

3.1   This section describes how we conducted the vacancy filling benchmarking study. It covers:

O   aims and objectives
O   team composition
O   measurement, research and analysis
O   relationships with benchmarking partners.


### AIMS AND OBJECTIVES

3.2   The vacancy filling benchmarking study was commissioned specifically to address identified weaknesses in the vacancy filling process. We therefore aimed to capture information on the current vacancy filling process to inform decision making and compare our processes internally across our nine regions and head office. Then, with the best practices in other organizations, we aimed to make our system more efficient and effective. Our stated objective was to 'radically reduce the elapsed time taken to fill a vacancy from the current average of 12 weeks'.

3.3     However as this was the first time benchmarking had been applied to a major HR area we also wanted to learn more about its use and the benefits it could bring to future reviews of HR processes. Fortunately during the project an opportunity presented itself for us to take part in a Consortium Study to look at the applicability of benchmarking to HR. We grasped this opportunity and joined the consortium so that we could share experiences with other Civil Service organizations that were using benchmarking in HR, so that we could learn more about its use.

3.4     We developed a project plan based on: our key objectives; the scope of the project which we had decided to limit to internal vacancy filling from advert to successful candidate taking up post; and the timescale for the project which was eight months from scoping to the delivery of recommendations. We included within the project plan all key activities, milestones and deadlines (see appendix 2).

3.5     This plan proved useful in identifying and securing resources for the project.

3.6     The project plan was regularly reviewed during the project in checkpoint meetings to take account of uncertainties and factors outside of our control, e.g. the project manager being taken ill and going on long term sick leave.

## MEET THE TEAM!

3.7     The vacancy filling benchmarking study team consisted of:

- ○ *project sponsor* – Director of HR: provided a high level steer for the project and was kept involved and informed throughout so that he could see the advantages of the approach and changes proposed
- ○ *project manager* – Deputy Head of Personnel: management of the project plan and interfacing with senior management
- ○ *project leader/policy adviser* – day-to-day management of the project and advice on the links and implications for related pieces of work. This person represented the policy unit who would ultimately be responsible for delivering the recommendations from the project

○ *project coordinator/practitioner* – provided the essential administrative support to the project and organized key activities in the project plan. This person also represented vacancy filling practitioners, i.e. those who support and undertake vacancy filling in ES regions

○ *internal benchmarking consultant* – provided a link with other process and benchmarking initiatives in ES, ES benchmarking expertise and acted as a 'gateway' to information from the division and Benchmarking Centre

○ *external personnel consultant* – provided internal facilitation and support to the project including research. She was fully integrated into the project team and provided expertise on HR reviews and research.

3.8    The project manager spent 0.5 days a week on the project; the project leader two days a week. The project coordinator was full time on the project. The internal consultant supported the project on a full-time basis for four months and the internal benchmarking consultant supported the project on an ad hoc basis as required.

3.9    Team members were chosen on the basis of their stake, expertise, skills and ability to work as part of a team to achieve a specific objective in a short timescale.

3.10   In addition to the core team we involved other people to provide advice and support to the project. These included:

○ *external consultant* – to provide expertise on benchmarking, training and to challenge our findings and assumptions

○ *ES cost adviser* – to advise us on data collection methods and cost information

○ *policy team* – to provide advice on related policies and to undertake some of the internal benchmarking activity

○ *vacancy filling working group* – a group that represented key stakeholders to test out our findings and emerging proposals

○ *regional vacancy filling implementers* – a group that represents regional personnel sections to advise on the practicalities of our emerging proposals

○ *Cabinet Office Consortium* – to share our findings and use of benchmarking to facilitate joint learning.

3.11   The core team received comprehensive training in the theory and use of benchmarking provided by the external consultant. They also received a tool kit consisting of good practice tips and techniques to help them undertake the study. In addition individual members of the team in discussions with either the project manager or leader identified and acted on their own development needs. An example of this was self-learning and mentoring on project management for the project coordinator. Early in the project we also identified a team deficiency in IT skills and attempted to overcome this through development. However, timescales restricted our ability to overcome the problem through training, so we had to utilize the skills of those in the wider team, e.g. external consultant.

3.12 Those providing advice to the project were fully briefed on the use of benchmarking and were given presentations regularly on the emerging outcomes from the project.

## UNDERSTAND YOUR OWN PROCESS BEFORE YOU COMPARE IT WITH OTHERS!

3.13 The first stage of our study involved the mapping of the vacancy filling process from end to end using IDEF/O. This gave us a better understanding of the process we were examining as we were able to identify the key processes, mechanisms and resources used to fill vacancies and the controls that influence the operation of the vacancy filling system. The IDEF/O map produced can be found at appendix 3.

3.14 We tested this model out on regional practitioners at a meeting and during visits to the regions and amended it slightly to take account of the feedback received.

3.15 This stage in itself proved to be useful in that we were able to identify the controls that were not open to challenge, e.g. equal opportunities legislation and those that were, e.g. ES policy on the completion of application forms. It also proved useful in getting regions to examine their practices and to take steps to improve them.

3.16 The process map also helped in the design of a questionnaire we used to identify potential benchmarking partners and in structuring the areas and questions to be covered on our visits.

3.17 Building on the information we had already established from the evaluation of internal vacancy filling and customer feedback, we then designed instruments to capture data on the operation of the internal vacancy filling system. We decided to use a variety of data collection methods with the emphasis being on getting the required data in the simplest way possible to ensure that our data collection did not become too resource intensive and burdensome for regions. We therefore modified existing monitoring questionnaires to collect information on the elapsed time, equal opportunities and the resources consumed by the system. We also identified any gaps and bridged these through the use of estimation techniques – questionnaires and telephone interviews.

3.18    We drew all this information together and used a bespoke Data Ease package to analyse the hard data.

3.19    The data gathered helped us identify the areas that were consuming the greatest amount of resource, namely the application stage 7.4 hours per applicant and the job specification stage 6.4 hours per specification. It also allowed us to determine the overall elapsed time which was 12 weeks and the areas that made the most significant contribution to that time, as well as differences in performance between regions which helped when comparing practices.

3.20    As a result we were able to identify the overall impact of the identified weaknesses on vacancy filling performance and consequently, by associating these to people's time and therefore cost, were able to determine the potential impact on organizational performance. We presented these findings in an interim report to senior management to highlight the issues. This helped show the importance of the study and benchmarking approach.

3.21    We then visited all nine ES regions and head office to share this information with regional practitioners and to identify best practices. On the visits we talked to key stakeholders and people that had been involved in vacancy filling using a structured interview to gather information.

3.22    It was reassuring to find that all regions were following a standard procedure and that the differences in performance were mainly due to better administrative practices. As a result of our visits more ES people became involved in the project and aware of the use of benchmarking and we were able to identify good practices that could help improve and streamline the process.

3.23    As a result of internal benchmarking we were able to encourage ES regions to adopt some of the practices that were being used by the better performing regions, e.g. vacancy plans. ES regions also used it as an impetus to look at their own procedures and make improvements. As a consequence the average elapsed time for filling a vacancy reduced by two weeks to 10 weeks!

## CHOOSING BENCHMARKING PARTNERS

3.24    We conducted extensive research, using journals, information from The Benchmarking Centre and the research facility in the Institute of Personnel and Development Library in order to identify public and private sector organizations that would be suitable comparators. We also made use of the knowledge that existed already in ES including a list of organizations that had already shown a commitment to benchmarking through an involvement in an earlier ES project.

3.25    We were mainly looking for organizations that would help us achieve our stated objective of reducing the elapsed time for filling vacancies and were aware from our research that the average elapsed time in companies was around 9–12 weeks which was very similar to ES. We also wanted to identify companies who used fewer resources to fill vacancies than ES and were committed to a robust, quality system. However we were also aware of the need to do some 'breakthrough' thinking so were also keen not to limit ourselves solely to organizations that were totally comparable to ES in their ways of working.

3.26    We did, however, concentrate our research on organizations that:

○    were comparable in size and geographical dispersion
○    had a changing organizational structure
○    had diversity within job types
○    had a degree of redeployment within the organization
○    filled a significant number of vacancies per annum
○    had an equal opportunities policy.

3.27    We felt that these considerations would be important when making comparisons of processes, but more importantly when selling the changes to others in ES. We were proved right on both assumptions, but particularly the latter.

3.28    We then developed a detailed questionnaire based on our process map, internal analysis and research which consisted of a good mix of both qualitative and quantitative questions. It covered areas such as: elapsed time for the process and each of its component parts; numbers of vacancies filled; costs; performance measures used; quality indicators; and the effort put into the process by HR, line managers and applicants. A copy of the questionnaire can be found at appendix 4.

3.29    Prior to sending out the questionnaire to our potential benchmarking partners we piloted it on people in ES and on a small number of external organizations. We then revised the questionnaire to take account of their comments, e.g. rewording some ambiguous questions and reducing the number of questions.

3.30    We sent out 44 questionnaires. Of these 20 were completed and returned (a response rate of 45 per cent)

3.31    We utilized the skills and expertise of our external consultant to undertake a detailed analysis of the responses using an Excel Package. He provided us with summary data presented in chart and graphical form for ease of use.

3.32    Three members of the project team independently analysed the questionnaires to identify organizations that would be suitable to benchmark against. Interestingly, there was a high degree of match between the three lists that were produced.

3.33   The team was surprised to find that the questionnaires did not reveal an organization with significantly better elapsed times for the process overall. We therefore focused our attention on those companies that had better process times for the individual stages, e.g. apply, sift, etc., and that appeared to use fewer resources than ES to fill vacancies.

3.34   We identified five organizations to visit: one Civil Service; one ex public sector; one private financial sector; one private multi-national; and one private retail.

3.35   However, we also decided to encourage a more radical approach to the selection of partners and involved personnel practitioners in a creative thinking exercise to identify a process that was similar to vacancy filling, i.e. 'getting the right things in the right place at the right time'. This produced a number of ideas, for example a fast food chain, tyre fitting and shelf filling in a supermarket. As a result we decided to compare our vacancy filling process with the shelf filling process of a successful supermarket.

## MEETING OUR BENCHMARKING PARTNERS

3.36   In all of our dealings with potential and actual benchmarking partners we followed the principles and ethics as set out in the published Benchmarking Code of Conduct.

3.37   Once we had decided on our short list of benchmarking partners we contacted our contact in the organization to set up a meeting. During this initial telephone conversation we outlined the nature of our study, what we would like their involvement to be and what we considered the benefits for them to be. We stressed that all information would be treated in confidence.

3.38   We were pleased that all were more than willing to meet with us to discuss their processes, although the supermarket did seem surprised that we wanted to find out about shelf filling rather than vacancy filling within their organization.

3.39   We confirmed our telephone agreement in writing, as well as giving the organizations some more information on ES, the areas we wished to explore in the meeting and a copy of our questions.

3.40   Two to three members of the team visited each organization as we wanted to ensure that we had enough knowledge, not only of the process, but of ES business generally. Also we needed one person to take notes while the other(s) asked questions.

3.41 At the meeting, we once again explained the purpose, stressed how the information would be treated in confidence or if it was to be used asked for their permission and encouraged them to see it as a reciprocal arrangement, i.e. we could learn from each other. We used a structured interview brief (appendix 5) to gather the required information.

3.42 At the first meeting we were encouraged by the openness of our partners, but surprised by their lack of interest in our arrangements. We therefore ensured in future meetings that we covered areas of interest to the partnering organization other than vacancy filling, e.g. one organization showed an interest in our competence framework.

3.43 We captured the key points from the visits on an interview record form. After each visit a debriefing session was held and the information from this and the record form was summarized for the rest of the team in writing and at meetings.

3.44 At the end of each meeting we thanked our partners for their time and involvement and agreed with them how we might maintain the relationship, including giving them a commitment to keep them informed of the outcomes from the project.

3.45 We have since maintained our relationships by sending every organization that completed a questionnaire a high level summary of our findings (see appendix 6) and each company we visited a copy of the Cabinet Office Consortium Project Report that included our case study. We have also 'left the door open' for further benchmarking, although as yet none of the companies have approached us to pursue this further. However, we intend building on the relationships within a current review of our recruitment practices.

## RESULTS

4.1 This section looks at the outcomes from our benchmarking study in terms of how we arrived at and implemented changes to vacancy filling; and the lessons we have learnt and how we will take account of these in future.

### 'WHAT A LOT WE HAVE GOT'

4.2 The benchmarking team were surprised at the amount of information they had gleaned from the visits to external organizations. All of it was summarized in a format that could be used by the whole team when developing proposals.

4.3    In order to determine best practices from different practices and to decide on what could be used in ES to improve vacancy filling arrangements we held a number of meetings where we looked at each of the key stages in filling a vacancy to:

O    identify how other organizations conduct that process differently to ES
O    identify 'best' practices
O    determine the benefits and drawbacks of each approach.

4.4    We utilized both the external consultant and our internal cost adviser to challenge our thinking both in terms of the emerging proposals and the rationale for maintaining the status quo in certain areas.

4.5    Through the use of a number of techniques, e.g. Critical Examination Matrix, Brainstorming and decision analysis we were able to develop a number of options that would help us achieve our objective. The key themes that emerged from this analysis were:

O    the use of IT to speed up the process for filling vacancies and reduce the time spent on administration
O    devolving greater responsibility to the line which would streamline the process and secure ownership of the system
O    providing additional support to help managers undertake their responsibilities and reduce administration
O    better planning
O    greater flexibility in the way candidate information is presented.

4.6    These themes formed the basis of our proposals for improvement which we arrived at by producing a 'Best Practice' Model (appendix 7) which enabled us to evaluate each proposal to ensure it fitted with the overall strategy and ES culture. We found that transporting practices straight from an organization into ES did not work. Instead, we had to look at the practice(s) and examine how they could best work in ES. This proved invaluable when selling the proposals to senior management and in allowing us to fit our proposals for vacancy filling alongside other significant changes being introduced in ES, e.g. a new ES IT communications system.

4.7    We were surprised by the general consensus within the team towards the 'best practice model', which could potentially reduce the elapsed time from advertisement to successful candidate taking up post to seven weeks and the proposals that underpinned it. However, we were well aware that we needed to build a consensus among stakeholders if we were to be successful in introducing the changes.

4.8    We had already established effective two-way communications with our key stakeholders through regular communications on the project and specific working groups. However, we had not involved them in some of the radical thinking which had led to some of the proposals and therefore needed to convince them of the benefits.

4.9    We have gained commitment to our proposals in a number of ways, namely:

○    regular updates and a presentation to the Director of HR to gain his commitment to the proposals. He was 'delighted' with the outcomes and has become an advocate of benchmarking as a result

○    a report to the senior decision-making body outlining our findings and the rationale for change. Again, this gained widespread approval both in terms of the approach taken and the proposals

○    presentations to groups representing users of the system and regional personnel managers. Here we came across the first real resistance to our proposals. Although the majority were accepted, our proposal aimed at removing personnel from the interview was opposed and they also pointed out some weaknesses we had missed in one other proposal. We refined that proposal and assured them on the other that if users generally were opposed to the proposal, we would look at either refining or dropping it

○    an article in *Inside ES*, the official ES newsletter to publicize the outcome of the study and the use of benchmarking

○    a large-scale consultation exercise where all the proposals (including their benefits and drawbacks) were put to ES people to get their comments and approval.

4.10    As a result of all this activity we have built a consensus around the majority of our proposals and senior management are committed to making the changes happen.

## WHAT HAS BEEN IMPLEMENTED?

4.11    Through regular communications and the involvement of key stakeholders we have been able to encourage gradual improvements in the way we fill vacancies based on the best practices identified through benchmarking. Regions have introduced better planning mechanisms, e.g. the use of a vacancy plan is now widespread; they have tightened up their procedures, e.g. release policy and have started to make more use of IT, e.g. in administrative procedures. As a result, we know from our monitoring arrangements that the average elapsed time has dropped to just over nine weeks (it was 12 weeks at the start of the study).

4.12 We have also developed a detailed implementation plan for the rest of the proposals which takes us right through to April 1998 when we intend extending the new, improved vacancy filling arrangements to everyone in ES.

4.13 We have run a number of tests of the new method of applying for vacancies and these have indicted a reduction of over 50 per cent on the time taken by applicants to complete their application.

4.14 We are now awaiting the outcome of the large consultation exercise before pressing ahead with the rest of our proposals, although the full benefits of some will be delayed due to timescales for the introduction of changes to other ES procedures, e.g. the new communications system which we intend using for advertising vacancies.

4.15 We have continued to monitor our vacancy filling arrangements throughout the study and are aware of the improvements in the elapsed time as a result. However, we have also reviewed our performance measures/benchmarks as a result of the study and developed a number of measures and a system for collecting information which will tell us whether the changes have had the desired effect and whether the system in the long term has improved as a result of them (appendix 8).

## WHAT HAVE WE LEARNED?

4.16 One of the main reasons we embarked on an in-depth benchmarking study such as this was to learn more about process benchmarking and in particular its applicability to HR. This is one of the reasons why we volunteered to become part of the Cabinet Office Consortium. We therefore documented the learning we got from the project during our regular check-point meetings.

4.17 The learning we have gained from our involvement in the study can be described under three headings:

- *organization* – what we learned about ES and our process as a result of benchmarking
- *benchmarking* – what we learned about benchmarking as a result of doing it
- *people* – what did individuals gain and what did we learn about teamwork.

### Organization

4.18 Our survey and visits to comparator organizations revealed that:

○ ES fills its vacancies as quickly as most broadly comparable organizations, but there remains significant scope for improvement

○ ES is far more aware of the actual performance of its vacancy filling system, which is exemplified by our knowledge of times and costs which were lacking elsewhere, but tends to focus much more on cost and efficiency measures than external organizations

○ personnel policies and procedures such as vacancy filling in other organizations tend to reflect the culture of the organization and are shaped by its philosophy towards managing people. This is less so in ES.

## Benchmarking

4.19    We learnt the following from the approach we took to benchmarking a HR area:

○ securing the right resources and the right amount of them is important. We feel that the size of our team, the support available and the ability of our team members were major factors in the success of the project. However, resources did take longer than expected to secure because of the need to weigh up the benefits against other priorities; this therefore needs to be built into the plan

○ it is vital that policy owners, practitioners and customers are involved and feel involved in the project. We did this through regular communications and working groups, yet still faced some resistance to some of our final proposals as they had not been involved in their development

○ consideration should always be given to internal benchmarking before going external. We were able to identify improvements that helped us achieve our objective and as a result were better informed when we went on the external visits

○ it is important to have a benchmarking project plan, but equally important to modify the plan as needed

○ comparator organizations may not apply the same measures to their own process: consequently you may need to rely on individual's perceptions of the process. We had to rely on structured interviews for our data as we were unable to observe the process as you may be able to in manufacturing for example

○ be prepared to identify best practices from a range of organizations, including those that may not be 'best in class'. We will never know whether we did actually compare ourselves to 'best in class'.

○ looking at unrelated, but comparable processes can help break mind blocks. For example, the comparison with supermarket shelf filling highlighted three approaches that could be applied to vacancy filling: different processes for different goods; daily orders for some goods; and optimizing stock levels, e.g. waiting lists

O  don't be too ambitious with the timescales for implementation. Build time for consensus building and testing into the implementation plan. We were initially hoping to have a new system in by the end of the summer 1997, but have now adopted a staged implementation over a longer timescale.

## People

4.20  We were fortunate in that the team gelled very well from the start and members were supportive of each other. The importance of this became very apparent as the project progressed, particularly when the project manager was taken ill and went on long-term sick leave. Members of the project team quickly rearranged responsibilities and ensured project outcomes were delivered.

4.21  During the project we did become aware of a lack of IT skills among the team which could not be addressed through training. We therefore had to utilize the skills of our external consultant. In future, we would take account of this requirement in the initial team selection.

4.22  All team members felt that they had gained a great deal from the project, including:

O  benchmarking skills
O  representational skills
O  data collection and analysis
O  increased confidence.

4.23  One member of the team on applying for a new position in the organization, said 'I would never have had the confidence to go for this without benchmarking.'

4.24  Overall the team were surprised by the effectiveness of the benchmarking approach and the 'spin offs' for the organization and themselves. This was perhaps best summed up by one team member who at the start of the project had described benchmarking as 'another management fad' and who at the end of the study when reminded of this, then stated 'I was wrong, it really does work'.

4.25  We have captured this learning for ourselves and will use it in other projects and for the organization and wider Civil Service in a publicized case study.

**HOW HAVE WE TAKEN THE LEARNING FORWARD?**

4.26    We have been sharing the learning from our benchmarking study with the wider HR community and the organization as a whole to encourage its use in other applications.

4.27    We have done this through a series of presentations to HR divisional managers, team leaders in personnel and practitioners, and an article in the ES newsletter. In these we have used our experience of benchmarking to outline the approach and to share our learning and good practices. As a result, benchmarking is going to be used in a review of one of our other major HR areas – recruitment – and is being considered for use in other areas. Awareness of the approach in ES generally has been raised as a result of the article.

4.28    We are also promoting the learning in the wider community by co-running workshops with the cabinet office for Civil Servants on the use of benchmarking in HR and planned presentations to the Cabinet Office Conference and articles for The Benchmarking Centre.

4.29    We plan to continue monitoring the effectiveness of our vacancy filling arrangements once they have been changed and intend reviewing the new arrangements after six months and as part of that review once again comparing ourselves against practices elsewhere.

4.30    We are convinced that this 'is not the end of our journey, only the beginning'.

Nick Parker
ES Personnel Division
Ground Floor, Block A
Porterbrook House
Pear Street
Sheffield S11

## APPENDIX 1: BENCHMARKING IN ES

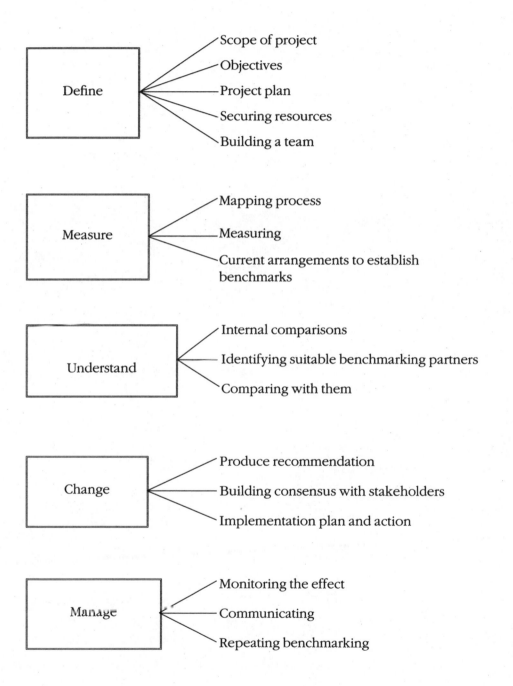

# APPENDIX 2: BENCHMARKING PROJECT PLAN

OPS Consortium Project Aim — To explore the use of the benchmarking as a tool to improve human resource practices. Learn more about benchmarking generally and about the techniques it involves.

ES Project Aim — To benchmarking against the 'best in class' with a view to radically reducing the time it takes to fill ES vacancies.

## ACTIVITIES AND OUTPUTS

**Stage 1**

Set up Consortium Project

| | Feb | March | April | May | June | July | Aug | Sept | Oct |
|---|---|---|---|---|---|---|---|---|---|
| Identify potential benchmarking topics. | I | | | | | | | | |
| Obtain OPS agreement to ES involvement in consortium. | I | | | | | | | | |
| Agree ground rules and funding arrangements. | I | | | | | | | | |
| Represent participating Departments in sifting and shortlisting of tenderers, interviewing shortlisted tenderers and selecting successful tenderer. | I | | | | | | | | |
| Shortlist potential benchmarking topics. | I | | | | | | | | |
| Represent ES at 1st consortium meeting. | I | | | | | | | | |
| Agree ES sphere of involvement. | I | | | | | | | | |
| Negotiate release of project resources. | I | I | | | | | | | |
| Arrange project initiation meeting. | I | I | | | | | | | |

X   Checkpoint meetings
●   Highlight reports
I   Completed activity
---   Ongoing Activity

| Feb | March | April | May | June | July | Aug | Sept | Oct |
|-----|-------|-------|-----|------|------|-----|------|-----|
| | | | | | | | | |
| | | | | | | | | |
| | | | | | | | | |
| | | | | | | | | |
| | | | | | | | | |
| | | | | | | | | |
| | | | | | | | | |
| | | | | | | | | |

**Stage 2**

Analysis

- Analyse the ES vacancy filling process to ensure that internal practices and processes are fully understood.

- Produce and validate vacancy filling process maps.

- Identify links with existing studies/projects.

- Review recent internal surveys/research to identify advantages/disadvantages of the current vacancy filling system.

- Identify which existing policies impact on speed of vacancy filling and who owns those policies.

- Establish benchmark for comparison with outside organizations.

**Stage 3**

Identify and visit benchmark partners

- Conduct research to identify 5 partners, including private and public sector organizations that are 'best in class' at vacancy filling and fill their vacancies more quickly than us.

- Produce aide-memoire for questions to be asked during visits to benchmark partners.

- Arrange visits to 5 benchmark partners.

- Conduct visits.

- Record outcomes.

| Feb | March | April | May | June | July | Aug | Sept | Oct |
|-----|-------|-------|-----|------|------|-----|------|-----|
|     |       |       |     |      |      |     |      |     |
|     |       |       |     |      |      |     |      |     |
|     |       |       |     |      |      |     |      |     |
|     |       |       |     |      |      |     |      |     |
|     |       |       |     |      |      |     |      | X   |
|     |       |       |     |      |      |     |      | X   |

**Stage 4**

Analyse Data, identify options and make proposals

- Analyse and discuss data emerging from 3 earlier stages. Seek IT specialist input if necessary.
- Identify and record main options for change
- Cost options and asses their feasibility.
- Agree lead option (consult as necessary)
- Write up lead option, including plans to bridge performance gaps between ES and the best in class.
- Produce case study for inclusion in OPS consortium final report.
- Produce Interim Project Report (by 31 August 1996).

**Stage 5**

- Informally consult stakeholders and relevant policy makers to identify potential friends and enemies.
- Agree implementation plan.
- Produce 'Final' Project Report (by 7 October 1996)
- Implement changes.
- Monitor results.
- Develop, if appropriate, a strategy of continuous improvement through benchmarking.

# APPENDIX 3: IDEF/O LEVEL 1 DIAGRAM

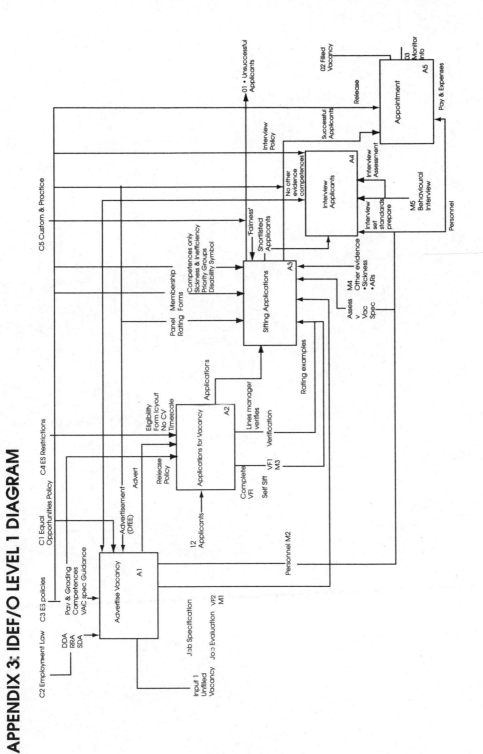

## APPENDIX 4: VACANCY FILLING PROCESS SURVEY 1996

*Employment* ✳ *Service*

**Employment Service**
Porterbrook House
7 Pear Street
Sheffield
S11 8JF

June 1996

# Vacancy Filling Process Survey 1996

Dear

The Employment Service is currently involved in a human resource
benchmarking project with other government departments. As part of that project we are looking to benchmark our internal vacancy filling process with the aim of radically reducing the
time it takes to fill vacancies.

Our current vacancy filling process has been in place since April 1994. An external evaluation
of the process by the Institute for Employment Studies confirmed that it has many strong features in that it is competence based, focused on job and business needs, objective, and
involves the vacancy holder in decisions. However, we would like to examine further the
possibility of reducing the time it takes us to fill vacancies. We have already examined our
processes and collected data on the time and costs of filling vacancies using the competence
based approach.

We are now seeking partners in the public and private sectors who are willing to share information on vacancy filling with us. Through our research we have identified you as a comparable and best practice organisation in this area and are therefore asking you to participate in
our study. Any information that you are willing to share will be treated with the strictest of
confidence. If you decide to take part in this survey, we will provide you with a top level
analysis and summary of the findings.

If you are willing to participate I would be grateful if you would complete the following questionnaire and return it in the pre-paid envelope by 21 June. Following on from this initial data
gathering exercise we may, with your agreement, arrange a follow up meeting to discuss your
response in more detail.

If you have any questions regarding the questionnaire or project please do not hesitate to ring:
**Wendy Pedley on 0181 680 1828.**

Thanking you in anticipation for your time and trouble.

**Mike Pender**
**Head of Equal Opportunities and Human Resources Projects**

1    Organization name    _____

       Contact name    _____  Tel No.   _____

       Address    _____

                        _____

       Name and position of person, to whom the results of the   _____
       survey should be sent (*if different from above*)

2    Which of the following apply within your organization? (*Please tick*)

       a ☐ a stated vacancy filling process
       b ☐ a different process for the filling of key/urgent jobs
       c ☐ a stated equal opportunities policy
       d ☐ an identified stock/pool of suitable candidates for future vacancies

3    Which, if any, of the following do you use to measure the success of your vacancy filling process? (*Please tick*)

       a ☐ service level agreements      h ☐ length of time a person remains in the same job
       b ☐ time taken to fill vacancies      i ☐ vacancies per annum as a percentage of employees
       c ☐ cost of filling vacancies        j ☐ number of people involved in the process
       d ☐ line manager satisfaction       k ☐ percentage of vacancies filled from first advert
       e ☐ applicant/candidate satisfaction   l ☐ number of terminations
       f ☐ appointees performance in the job  h ☐ other (*please give details*)
       g ☐ staff turnover

                                         _____

                                         _____

| 4  How do you feel the following characterize your vacancy filling arrangements (*Please tick*) | Agree strongly | Agree | Not sure | Disagree | Disagree strongly |
| --- | --- | --- | --- | --- | --- |
| a  HR/Personnel have total responsibility for the vacancy filling process? | ☐ | ☐ | ☐ | ☐ | ☐ |
| b  the line have total responsibility for the vacancy filling process? | ☐ | ☐ | ☐ | ☐ | ☐ |
| c  the process is administered by a central HR/Personnel department? | ☐ | ☐ | ☐ | ☐ | ☐ |

| | Agree strongly | Agree | Not sure | Disagree | Disagree strongly |
|---|---|---|---|---|---|
| d   the process is administered by the line? | ☐ | ☐ | ☐ | ☐ | ☐ |
| e   the process is administered by decentralized (regional) Personnel departments | ☐ | ☐ | ☐ | ☐ | ☐ |
| f   the recruitment function is driven by manpower planning which allows for the forecasting of future vacancies? | ☐ | ☐ | ☐ | ☐ | ☐ |
| g   the filling of vacancies is only for specific posts? | ☐ | ☐ | ☐ | ☐ | ☐ |
| h   the release dates for internal candidates are negotiated between all parties? | ☐ | ☐ | ☐ | ☐ | ☐ |
| i   release dates for internal candidates are enforced so that jobs are filled quickly? | ☐ | ☐ | ☐ | ☐ | ☐ |

5   Do you operate a vacancy filling process that is only open (initially) to internal candidates:

   Yes ☐   No ☐

**If yes, please complete the following questions giving separate answers for your internal process (vacancies open to internal candidates only, initially) and your external process (vacancies open to internal candidates and/or external candidates).**

**If No, please complete the questions giving answers for the external process only.**

6   Which of the following criteria is your process based on: (*Please tick*)

| | Internal process | External process |
|---|---|---|
| a   Compentencies identified for each post | ☐ | ☐ |
| b   Experienced gained | ☐ | ☐ |
| c   Courses attended | ☐ | ☐ |
| d   Qualifications | ☐ | ☐ |
| e   Skills | ☐ | ☐ |
| f   Personal attributes | ☐ | ☐ |
| g   Performance reviews | ☐ | ☐ |
| h   Manager references | ☐ | ☐ |
| i   Other (*please describe*) | ☐ | ☐ |

_____

_____

7   What do you believe to be the percentage effort put into the process by the following and please also give time taken (in hours) by each if known:

|  | Internal process % effort | time taken (*hours*) | External process % effort | time taken (*hours*) |
|---|---|---|---|---|
| a  HR/Personnel | % | ——— | % | ——— |
| b  line manager | % | ——— | % | ——— |
| c  applicant | % | ——— | % | ——— |
| d  other (*please describe*) | % | ——— | % | ——— |
|  | ——————— | | ——————— | |
|  | ——————— | | ——————— | |
| TOTAL | 100% | ——— | 100% | ——— |

8   What is the average elapsed time taken (in weeks) from the notification of a vacancy to the successful person being in post? (*Please tick*)

|  | 0 - 6 | 6 - 9 | 9 - 11 | 11 - 13 | 13 - 15 | 15+ |
|---|---|---|---|---|---|---|
| Internal process (*weeks*) | ☐ | ☐ | ☐ | ☐ | ☐ | ☐ |
| External process (*weeks*) | ☐ | ☐ | ☐ | ☐ | ☐ | ☐ |

9   Please complete the following matrix giving the elapsed time taken for completion of each activity and tick if technology (IT) is used in the activity

|  | Internal process elapsed time taken (*calendar days*) | IT used | External process elapsed time taken (*calendar days*) | IT used |
|---|---|---|---|---|
| a  notification to advertisement | ——— | ☐ | ——— | ☐ |
| b  advertisement to closing date for application | ——— | ☐ | ——— | ☐ |
| c  sifting to selection | ——— | ☐ | ——— | ☐ |
| d  selection to person taking up post | ——— | ☐ | ——— | ☐ |
| b  other (*please describe*) | ——— | ☐ | ——— | ☐ |
|  | ——— | | | |

10   Which of the following does your process include: (*Please tick*)

|  | Internal | External |
|---|---|---|
| a  consideration of surplus internal people first | ☐ | ☐ |
| b  advertising of posts | ☐ | ☐ |
| c  application forms | ☐ | ☐ |

|  |  | Internal | External |
|---|---|---|---|
| d | CVs | ☐ | ☐ |
| e | references of suitability for job | ☐ | ☐ |
| f | assessment centres | ☐ | ☐ |
| g | tests and exercises | ☐ | ☐ |
| h | interviews | ☐ | ☐ |
| i | resource stock/pools from which suitable people can be picked to fill vacancies | ☐ | ☐ |
| j | other (*please describe*) ——————————— | ☐ | ☐ |

11    Please indicate, with a tick, the number of vacancies your organization filled in 1995:

|  | less than 250 | 251-750 | 751-1000 | 1001-1500 | 1501-2500 | over 2500 |
|---|---|---|---|---|---|---|
| Internal process | ☐ | ☐ | ☐ | ☐ | ☐ | ☐ |
| External process | ☐ | ☐ | ☐ | ☐ | ☐ | ☐ |

12    What is the average number of applicants you have per vacancy? (*please tick most appropriate*)

|  | less than 5 | 6-10 | 11-20 | 21-50 | 51-100 | 101-200 | over 200 |
|---|---|---|---|---|---|---|---|
| Internal process | ☐ | ☐ | ☐ | ☐ | ☐ | ☐ | ☐ |
| External process | ☐ | ☐ | ☐ | ☐ | ☐ | ☐ | ☐ |

13    Please indicate the size of your organization's budget for vacancy filling in 1995: (*please tick*)

| less than £100,000 | £100,001-£200,000 | £200,001-£500,000 | £500,001-£750,000 | £750,001-£1000,000 | over £1000,000 |
|---|---|---|---|---|---|
| ☐ | ☐ | ☐ | ☐ | ☐ | ☐ |

14    If you have stated objectives/aims for your vacancy filling process please outline them:

_____

_____

_____

_____

_____

_____

15    What do you believe are the key strengths of your process (ie what do you do well)?

1    _____

_____

2    _____

_____

3    _____

_____

4    _____

_____

Other    _____

_____

16     Please feel free to make any additional comments, e.g. are you planning to make
       any significant changes, have you recently invested in technology in this area, etc.
       (*continue on a separate sheet if necessary*)

       _____
       _____
       _____
       _____
       _____
       _____
       _____

**Thank you for the time and trouble taken in completing this questionnaire.
All information provided will be held in the strictest confidence.**

# APPENDIX 5: INTERNAL VACANCY FILLING

BENCHMARKING VISIT - 11.00 am FRIDAY 26TH JULY 1996

Nick Parker, Wendy Pedley, Yan Cursley

INTERNAL VACANCY FILLING

**Policies**

1    We have a stated vacancy filling policy covering our Management Pay-bands (Middle Management) which gives guidelines on:

   – drawing up a competency based vacancy specification
   – career development and operational moves
   – advertising a vacancy
   – the application stage
   – the sift stage
   – the interview stage
   – how to apply our policies of equal opportunities and ensure fair and open competition

**QUESTIONS FOR                (to be covered at the meeting)**

**From your questionnaire we know that you have a stated internal vacancy filling process and an Equal Opportunities policy.**

What policies do you have for internal vacancy filling?
Why do you have them?
What other policies/company practices influence the way you fill vacancies?
How do you ensure compliance with Equal Opportunities requirements?

**From your questionnaire we know that you measure the success of your vacancy filling by using a number of factors, i.e. service level agreements, line manager satisfaction.**

How do you measure these?
How do you use the information?
How much does it cost to fill an internal vacancy?

## Procedures

2     Our Head Office vacancies are advertised centrally by the Department of Education and Employment (DfEE) and are distributed to our offices throughout the country via a vacancy circular. Vacancies in Regions are advertised in a Regional Vacancy Notice either weekly or as the vacancy is notified.

Before a vacancy is advertised our Personnel Managers would identify surplus people who would be suitable and would need to be considered first. If none are identified the vacancy is advertised.

The Personnel Manager would determine the terms of the advertisement, i.e. whether the post could be opened to substantive people only; for promotion or detached duty terms. On receiving vacancy details from the line manager Personnel precis it and send it to the printers to be advertised in the next available circular. The circular is issued weekly and has a two week closing date. Applicants must ring us for an application form and a full job description on which to base their application. The pack we send also includes guidance on the completion of the application form and information on the salary structure. Each Region has a similar procedure but may vary it depending on resources available.

**QUESTIONS FOR**                    **(to be covered at the meeting)**

**From your questionnaire we know that the percentage effort put into the internal vacancy filling process by the line manager is 60%.**

What responsibilities do line managers have?
What tasks and activities do they undertake?

**From your questionnaire we know that you electronically advertise jobs to all staff and that you filled between 251 to 750 vacancies by internal candidates in 1995.**

How do you advertise?
What does the advert include?
How wide is the distribution?
How do applicants apply for jobs?
Who determines eligibility?
What constraints do you have?

3     At the closing date we prepare the papers for the sift. This involves copying the application forms to all sift panel members (line manager,

Personnel representative) and ensuring details like sick records are available. The pack also includes sift guidance and reminds them of the constraints we have to work within, i.e. competency based sifting; Equal Opportunities policies; applications from surplus people that must be considered first, people with disabilities who apply and meet the minimum criteria for the job are guaranteed an interview; promotion bans.

**QUESTIONS FOR                  (to be covered at the meeting)**

**From your questionnaire we know that sifts and interviews are conducted within 5-10 days, that you consider surplus people first and that you apply a flexible use of candidate information.**

How are surplus people considered, i.e. apply before everyone else, by guaranteeing an interview?
What do you sift/select applicants against?
How are the various types of candidate information used?
What methods do you use for sifting/selecting suitable applicants? e.g. Paper sift, interview.
Why do you use that particular method?
Who would be involved in the sifting process? What is their role?
Is there any particular reason for their involvement?
How many people would you put through each stage of your selection process per vacancy?
How are internal promotions handled – are they different from level transfers?
Do you have any constraints – if so what constraints do you have?

4     We try to include the date of the interviews in the advertisement. When interviews are arranged all contact must be done by Personnel via the applicant's line manager (for Head Office applicants) or via the Regional personnel department for applicants from others parts of the country. We may not approach the person direct.

**QUESTIONS FOR                  (to be covered at the meeting)**

**Do you have any such protocol regarding approaching applicants?**
**How do applicants find out the date of interview?**

5     Once the interview is arranged copies of the papers and interview guidance is sent to the interviewers (line manager, Personnel representative). The interviews are very structured with each interviewer

testing a given competence(s). The
hensive records are kept. Records of
each interview and are used as a basi
who are unsuccessful at interview are
Again this would be issued and seen by
passed to the applicant. The Line Manag
with the applicant to hopefully improve
next time.

**QUESTIONS FOR                     (to be co**

**From your questionnaire we know that**
**your selection process.**

Who is involved in interviewing? Are all interv
What criteria do you interview against?
How are your interviews structured?
Does the make up of the interviewing panel d
opportunity?
If feedback is provided, what format does it take?

6    Once the decision has been made. The offer of the
relevant personnel department or line manager as a
date is then negotiated. Our line managers and/or
ments have the right of veto and can stop an applicatio
or can refuse release for a new post on operational gr

**QUESTIONS FOR                     (to be covered at the**

**From your questionnaire we know that it takes be**
**days from the decision being made to the succes**
**taking up post.**

Who is involved in the negotiations?
How are moves/transfers of people organized?
Are salaries predetermined or is this part of the negotiation p
Do you encounter any problems from the exporting mana
release for internal people?
Do your line managers/personnel departments have the right
on operational grounds?

7    If an applicant is unhappy with the result of the interview and
that their application has been prejudiced in some way they have
right to appeal. We have an established appeals procedure and
also time bound.

## APPENDIX 6: EMPLOYMENT SERVICE ANALYSIS OF BENCHMARKING DATA OBTAINED THROUGH EXTERNAL QUESTIONNAIRE

This document is available on application to:

Nick Parker
Policy Manager
Employment Service
Personnel Division
Ground Floor, Block A
Porterbrook House
Pear Street
Sheffield S11

Tel:  +44 (0) 114 259 6858
Fax: +44 (0) 114 259 6742

# APPENDIX 7: ES INTERNAL VACANCY FILLING, BEST PRACTICE MODEL

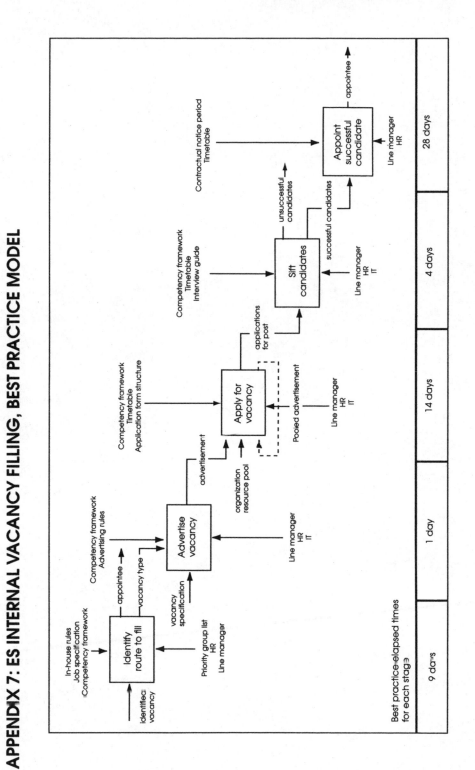

# APPENDIX 8: PERFORMANCE

| No. | Performance measure (PM)[1] | Aim(s) supported[2] | Measure(s) of achievement to support aims[3] | Interested stake-holder(s)[4] | Data source | Frequency of PM calculation | Current performance[5] | Target performance (where applicable) | Report reference[6] | Notes |
|---|---|---|---|---|---|---|---|---|---|---|
| 1 | Average elapsed time to fill a vacancy (from notification to successful applicant taking up post). | 3 | Reduce turnaround time for filling vacancies. | VH, A, PD. | Vacancy filling – monitoring information summary. | Quarterly. | 84 days (national av). | 49 days (national av.) | Para 2.14 | |
| 1.1 | Average elapsed time to produce and issue a vacancy specification. | As 1. | As 1. | VH, PD. | Vacancy filling – monitoring information summary (VF-MIS). | Quarterly. | 10 days (national av). | 2 days (national av) | Para 2.8 | Non-continuous monitoring (for one year only?). Will require an extra filed on the VF-MIS. |
| 1.2 | Average elapsed time from advert to offer being made. | As 1. | As 1. | VH, PD, A | Vacancy filling – monitoring information summary [?]. | Quarterly. | 57 days | 19 days | Para 2.14 | Non-continuous monitoring (for one year only?). Will require an extra filed on the VF-MIS. |
| 1.3 | Average elapsed time from offer being made to applicant taking up post. | As 1. | As 1. | PD. | Vacancy filling – monitoring information summary. | Quarterly. | 45 days (national max) – 27 days (national av). | 95% to be completed within 28 days | Para 2.13 | Non-continuous monitoring (for one year only?). |

| No. | Performance measure (PM)[1] | Aim(s) supported[2] | Measure(s) of achievement to support aims[3] | Interested stake-holder(s)[4] | Data source | Frequency of PM calculation | Current performance[5] | Target performance (where applicable) | Report reference[6] | Notes |
|---|---|---|---|---|---|---|---|---|---|---|
| 2 | Average time staff spend in filling a vacancy. | 4 | | PD. | Sum of 2.2 and 2.3. | Quarterly. | | | | |
| 2.1 | Average time vacancy holders spend in writing a vacancy specification. | As 2. | | VH, PD. | Data to be collected from a sample of vacancy holders [?]. | Quarterly. | 6.7 hours. | | Paras 2.8, 5.5-5.7 | Non-continuous monitoring (for one year only?). |
| 2.2 | Average time personnel spend in filling a vacancy. | As 2. | Managers carrying out more HR management activity. | PD. | Data to be collected from a sample of personnel staff [?]. | Quarterly. | 8.67 hours. | | | Non-continuous monitoring (for one year only?). |
| 2.3 | Average time vacancy holder spends in filling a vacancy. | As 2. | As 2.1. | VH, PD. | Data to be collected from a sample of vacancy holders [?]. | Quarterly. | Not known. | | | Non-continuous monitoring (for one year only?). |
| 2.4 | Average time applicants spend in completing the necessary application. | As 2. | | PD, A. | Individual monitoring form. | Quarterly. | 7.37 hours. | | Para 2.9 | Non-continuous monitoring (for one year only?). |

| No. | Performance measure (PM)[1] | Aim(s) supported[2] | Measure(s) of achievement to support aims[3] | Interested stake-holder(s)[4] | Data source | Frequency of PM calculation | Current performance[5] | Target performance (where applicable) | Report reference[6] | Notes |
|---|---|---|---|---|---|---|---|---|---|---|
| 2.4.1 | Average time short-listed applicants spend in completing the necessary application. | As 2. | | PD. | Individual monitoring form. | Quarterly. | 8.31 hours. | None. | | Non-continuous monitoring (for one year only?). The measure ensures that a reduced time at 2.4 does not reduce the effectiveness of the application. |
| 3 | Rejection rate of vacancy specifications. | ? | | PD, VH. | PDs to monitor. | Quarterly. | Not applicable/ known | <[?]% | | Non-continuous monitoring (for one year only?). |
| 4 | ES staffs' perception of the fairness of competence based vacancy filling process [measure required based on survey rating/score]. | 4 | More positive responses to the Regular Staff Survey. | PD, A. | ES Regular Attitude Survey. | Annually. | ? | | Para 2.11. | |

| No. | Performance measure (PM)[1] | Aim(s) supported[2] | Measure(s) of achievement to support aims[3] | Interested stake-holder(s)[4] | Data source | Frequency of PM calculation | Current performance[5] | Target performance (where applicable) | Report reference[6] | Notes |
|---|---|---|---|---|---|---|---|---|---|---|
| 5 | Line managers assessment of appointed applicants [performance measure required based on survey rating/score]. | 4 | More positive responses to the Regular Staff Survey. People performing to required standards of delivery. | PD. | Data to be collected from questionnaires sent to a sample of line managers. | Annually. | Not known. | | | Measures the effectiveness of the process to get the right person in the right job. |

1  Performance measures on 'equal opportunities' are not considered here.
2  From the 'ES Human Resource Strategy Statement' [draft] – undated. The aims of the strategy are to provide 1) people who perform to required standards of delivery; 2) an organization that encourages commitment; 3) the right number of people when and where they are needed, and 4) effectively managed teams and offices.
3  From the 'ES Human Resource Strategy Statement' [draft] – undated.
4  VH = vacancy holders; A = applicants; PD = personnel divisions (including RO and HO personnel staffs).
5  See PPSG 2/96 for details.
6  'MPB competence based vacancy filling: cost review and benchmarking exercise', PD2, (no date).

PART

*4*

# APPENDICES

# ACRONYMS AND ABBREVIATIONS

Acronyms abound in the world of business and particularly in areas related to quality. The following is a list of some of those most frequently used. Although it is by no means exhaustive it provides a good working knowledge for everyday usage.

| | |
|---|---|
| bpb | best practice benchmarking |
| bpr | business process re-engineering |
| ci | continuous improvement |
| tqm | total quality management |
| spc | statistical process control |
| cc | core competence |
| kbp | key business process |
| kpi | key performance indicator |
| csf | critical success factor |
| TBE | The Benchmarking Exchange |
| BMC | The Benchmarking Centre |
| sme | small- and medium-sized enterprises |
| DTI | Department of Trade and Industry |
| WCSN | World class standards network |
| BQF | British Quality Foundation |
| EFQM | European Foundation for Quality Management |
| EBPBA | European Best Practice Benchmarking Award™ |
| BQA | British Quality Award |
| EQA | European Quality Award |
| EC | European Commission |
| DGIII | Directorate General III (Industry) at the EC |
| nih | not invented here |
| wiifm | 'what's in it for me' |

APPENDIX

**II**

# USEFUL CONTACTS

While wishing to provide the most up-to-date information regarding contacts, the nature and pace of change is such that no sooner are details printed than they are out of date. Although the majority of the organizations listed below have email addresses and many have web sites, their details are subject to frequent change. Hence, it is suggested that you contact the Benchmarking Centre nearest to you to obtain current information. Alternatively, look up The UK Benchmarking Centre web site or telephone them.

## ENGLAND

The Benchmarking Centre Limited
Truscon House
11 Station Road
Gerrards Cross
Bucks UK
SL9 8ES
Tel.:        +44 1753 890070
Fax.:        +44 1753 893070
e: mail:      info@benchmarking.co.uk
Web site:    http:\\www.info@benchmarking.co.uk

Centre for Interfirm Comparison
Capital House
48 Andover Road
Winchester
Hampshire UK
SO23 7BH
Tel.:        +44 1962 844144
Fax.:        +44 1962 843180

PIMS Benchmarking Council
7th Floor
Moor House
119 London Wall
London
EC2Y 5ET
Tel.:       +44 171 628 1155
Fax.:       +44 171 628 2455

## BELGIUM

European Foundation for Quality Management
Avenue des Pleiades 19
B-1200 Brussels
Tel.:       +32 2 775 3511
Fax.:       +32 2 775 3535

## FINLAND

The Finnish Benchmarking Association
17A Teknikantie
Universidad de Navarra
021250 Espoo
Tel.:       +358 505571152
Fax.:       +3580 51122597

## FRANCE

Institut du Benchmarking (France)
8 Avenue Delcasse
75008 Paris
Tel.:       +33 1 5377 3560
Fax.:       +33 1 5377 3561

Le Benchmarking Club de Paris
116 Avenue abriel Peri
93585 Saint-Ouen
Paris
Tel.:       +01 40 11 87 08
Fax.:       +01 40 11 87 02

**GERMANY**

Benchmarking Center
Fraunhofer Institute
Theodorstrasse 1
D-90489 Nuernberg
Tel.:        +49 911 58879-88
Fax.:        +49 911 588 7933

Informationszentrum Benchmarking (IZB)
Fraunhofer Institute
Pascal Strasse 8-9
D-10587
Berlin
Tel.:        +49 303 9006258
Fax.:        +49 303 932503

**INDIA**

India Benchmarking Centre
Institute of Quality Ltd
K-4 Hauz Khas Enclave
New Delhi - 110 016
Tel.:        +91 11 6513270
Fax.:        +91 11 6512677

**ITALY**

The Benchmarking Club
Via Isonzo 42/C
00198 Rome
Tel.:        + 39 6 8413608
Fax.:        + 39 6 8442034

Benchmarking Council Italia
Via Cerva 1
20122 Milano 1
Tel.:        +39 2 7601 3030
Fax.:        +39 2 760 28476

## KOREA

Korean Benchmarking Centre
Suite 1104
Seochoworld Building
Seocho-Dong 1355-3
Seocho-Ku
Seoul
137–070
Tel.:        +82 255 377 34
Fax.:       +82 256 772 20

## SINGAPORE

Fuji-Xerox PSB Benchmarking Centre
Singapore Productivity and Standards Board
PSB Building
2 Bukit Merah Central
Singapore 159835
Fax.:       + 65 278 6666
Tel.:       + 65 278 6665/7

## SOUTH AFRICA

Benchmarking South Africa – Bensa
National Productivity Institute
PO Box 3971
7th Floor Prodinsa Building
Cor Beatrix & Pretorius Street
0001 Pretoria
Tel.:        + 27 12 341 1470
Fax.:       + 27 12 44 1866

## SWEDEN

The Swedish Institute for Quality
Benchmarking Service
Fabriksgatan 10
S-41250 Gothenburg
Tel.:        + 46 31351700
Fax.:       + 46 317730645

**USA**

American Productivity and Quality Center
123 North Post Oak Lane
3rd Floor
Houston
Texas 77024
Tel.:       +1 713 681 4020
Fax.:       +1 713 681 8578

The Quality Network Inc
Park Central Suite F
110 Linden Oaks Drive
Rochester
New York 14625-2832
Tel.:       +1 716 248 5712
Fax.:       +1 716 248 2940

SPI Council on Benchmarking
1030 Massachusetts Avenue
Cambridge
MA 02138
Tel.:       +1 908 953 9007
Fax.:       +1 908 953 9010

# FURTHER READING

Anderson, Bjorn and Pettersen, Per-Gaute (1996), *The Benchmarking Handbook*, London: Chapman & Hall.
A step-by-step instruction book following the problem solving process from a Scandinavian perspective. Includes checks lists, worksheets and case studies from Norwegian Winch Corporation, Statoil, Glamox and Pacific Bell.

Balm, G.J. (1992), *Benchmarking: A Practitioner's Guide for Becoming and Staying Best of the Best*, Schaumburg, Illinois: Quality Productivity Management Association .
A 'how to' book based on the experience at IBM's Rochester, Minnesota USA site. Explains the technique through the company's 15-step process. A practical guide in the American style.

Camp, Robert C. (1989), *Benchmarking: The Search for Industry Best Practices that Lead to Superior Performance*, Milwaukee, Wisconsin: ASQC Press.
Not the easiest to read, this was the first book on the subject, now a classic; it relates the experience of benchmarking at Xerox Corporation in the USA.

Camp, Robert C. (1995), *Business Process Benchmarking*, Milwaukee, Wisconsin: ASQC Quality Press.
More practical than Bob Camp's first book, this is an updated companion to it. Covers the Xerox benchmarking process, the leadership and management issues and five detailed US case studies. Broad in scope.

Codling, Sylvia (1992), *Best Practice Benchmarking*, Dunstable, Beds: Industrial Newsletter (republished 1995, Aldershot: Gower).
The first European book on the subject and the first to synthesize the

various approaches into the now classic 12-step methodology. Uncomplicated, non-academic and aimed at practitioners, answers all the basic questions and includes many snapshots and case studies of early benchmarking.

Hardjono, T.W., ten Have, S. and W.D. (1996), *The European Way to Excellence*, Brussels: Directorate General 111 Industry, European Commission European Quality Publications.
Based on actual case studies of 35 European manufacturing, service and public sector organizations, ranging in size from very small to large. The authors, management consultants with independent Dutch management consultancy, Berenschot, worked in close consultation with the case study writers to produce this fact-based analysis. It examines what quality management and the quest for excellence means to European organizations. It describes how they have managed both business and organizational challenges and paints a picture of the approaches chosen. The emphasis is on providing insights, rather than developing recipes or 'how to' models.

Lock, Dennis (ed.), *Handbook of Quality Management* 2nd edition, Aldershot: Gower .
Essential reference book comprising contributions from leading thinkers in the quality field. Encompasses quality policy and concepts, quality related costs and benefits, legislation and standards, quality organization and administration, quality in design and engineering, purchasing and materials handling, statistical process control, quality functions in manufacturing and participative quality improvement.

Leonard-Barton, Dorothy (1995), *Wellsprings of Knowledge*, Harvard: Harvard Business School Press.
An excellent book for those wishing to explore the concept of core competencies and understand how to exploit it. Not the easiest read but practical examples make it nevertheless enjoyable and worth persevering with.

Oakland, John S. (1989), *Total Quality Management*, Oxford: Butterworth-Heinemann Ltd.
For all those wondering what total quality management is all about, this is a well written and early classic which encompasses all the key points in a straightforward and uncluttered fashion.

Watson, Gregory H. (1993), *Strategic Benchmarking*, New York: John Wiley.
In its early days benchmarking was viewed purely as a practical mea-

surement tool. This book was arguably the first to broaden the concept into the strategic and learning arenas. Clear, straightforward and easy to read while also providing food for thought.

Zairi, M. (1996), *Effective Benchmarking,* London: Chapman & Hall.
A book of case studies from companies who have been benchmarking for some years and hence imbued with considerable experience of the up and downside. The book relates their deployment of benchmarking and processes to which it has been applied. Companies include Kodak Ltd, TNT Express, Royal Mail, Texal Instruments, Leeds Permanent Building Society and Northern Telecom among many others. This is an excellent book if you want to learn who else is doing benchmarking and how they are applying the technique.

Zairi, M. and Leonard, P. (1994), *Practical Benchmarking: The Complete Guide*, London: Chapman & Hall .
A comprehensive guide to the subject, its background and fit with TQM. Numerous examples and practical applications in a variety of functions, which includes an overview of various methodologies being used and the organizations promoting benchmarking. A practical 'who is doing it and where' rather than a 'how to' book.

# CODES OF CONDUCT

## ■ INTRODUCTION TO CODE OF CONDUCT FOR BENCHMARKING

The following codes have been developed to guide benchmarking activities between companies. The 'European Code' is an amended version of the earlier 'International Code' and takes special cognisance of European Community Law.

Neither code is binding in law, but all organizations conducting benchmarking agree, as a matter of principle and best practice, to adhere to the code. You should select whichever best suits your situation – there is very little difference between them – and ensure that your partners and team members all receive a copy of the same one.

## ■ THE INTERNATIONAL BENCHMARKING CODE OF CONDUCT

To contribute to efficient, effective and ethical benchmarking, individuals agree for themselves and their organization to abide by the following principles for benchmarking with other organizations.

1.  **Principle of Legality.** Avoid discussions or actions that might lead to or imply an interest in restraint of trade; market or customer allocation schemes; price fixing; dealing arrangements; bid rigging; bribery; or misappropriation. Do not discuss costs with competitors if costs are an element of pricing.
2.  **Principle of Exchange.** Be willing to provide the same level of information that you request in any benchmarking exchange.
3.  **Principle of Confidentiality**. Treat benchmarking interchange as something confidential to the individuals and organizations involved. Information obtained must not be communicated out-

side the partnering organizations without prior consent of participating benchmarking partners. An organization's participation in a study should not be communicated externally without their permission.

4.  **Principle of Use.** Use information obtained through benchmarking partnering only for the purpose of improvement of operations with the partnering companies themselves. External use or communication of a benchmarking partner's name with their data or observed practices requires permission of that partner. Do not, as a consultant or client, extend one company's benchmarking study findings to another without the first company's permission.

5.  **Principle of First Party Contact**. Initiate contacts, whenever possible, through a benchmarking contact designated by the partner company. Obtain mutual agreement with the contact on any hand off of communication or responsibility to other parties.

6.  **Principle of Third Party Contact.** Obtain an individual's permission before providing their name in response to a contact request.

7.  **Principle of Preparation.** Demonstrate commitment to the efficiency and effectiveness of the benchmarking process with adequate preparation at each process step, particularly, at initial partnering contact.

## ETIQUETTE AND ETHICS

In actions between benchmarking partners, the emphasis is on openness and trust. The following guidelines apply to both partners in a benchmarking encounter:

- In benchmarking with competitors, establish specific ground rules up front, e.g. 'We do not want to talk about those things that will give either of us a competitive advantage, rather, we want to see where we both can mutually improve or gain benefit.'
- Do not ask competitors for sensitive data or cause the benchmarking partner to feel that sensitive data must be provided to keep the process going.
- Use an ethical third party to assemble any blind competitive data, with inputs from legal counsel, for direct competitor comparisons.
- Consult with legal counsel if any information gathering procedure is in doubt, e.g. before contacting a direct competitor.
- Any information obtained from a benchmarking partner should be treated as internal privileged information.

- Do not:
  - disparage a competitor's business or operations to a third party
  - attempt to limit competition or gain business through the benchmarking relationship.

## BENCHMARKING EXCHANGE PROTOCOL

As the benchmarking process proceeds to the exchange of information, benchmarkers are expected to:

✓ Know and abide by the Benchmarking Code of Conduct.
✓ Have basic knowledge of benchmarking and follow a benchmarking process.
✓ Have determined what to benchmark, identified key performance variables, recognized superior performing companies, and completed a rigorous self-assessment.
✓ Have developed a questionnaire and interview guide, and will share these in advance if requested.
✓ Have the authority to share information.
✓ Work through a specified host and mutually agree on scheduling and meeting arrangements.
✓ Follow these guidelines in face-to-face site visits:
  - provide meeting agenda in advance
  - be professional, honest, courteous and prompt
  - introduce all attendees and explain why they are present
  - adhere to the agenda. Maintain focus on benchmarking issues
  - use language that is universal, not one's own jargon
  - do not share proprietary information without prior approval, from the proper authority, of both parties
  - share information about your process, if asked, and consider sharing study results
  - offer to set up a reciprocal visit
  - conclude meetings and visits on schedule.

## EUROPEAN BENCHMARKING CODE OF CONDUCT

### 1.0 Principle of preparation

1.1 Demonstrate commitment to the efficiency and effectiveness of benchmarking by being prepared prior to making an initial benchmarking contact.

1.2   Make the most of your benchmarking partner's time by being fully prepared for each exchange.

1.3   Help your benchmarking partners prepare by providing them with a questionnaire and agenda prior to benchmarking visits.

1.4   Before any benchmarking contact, especially the sending of questionnaires, take legal advice.

## 2.0   Principle of contact

2.1   Respect the corporate culture of partner organizations and work within mutually agreed procedures.

2.2   Use benchmarking contacts designated by the partner organization if that is its preferred procedure.

2.3   Agree with the designated benchmarking contact how communication or responsibility is to be delegated in the course of the benchmarking exercise. Check mutual understanding.

2.4   Obtain an individual's permission before providing their name in response to a contact request.

2.5   Avoid communicating a contact's name in open forum without the contact's prior permission.

## 3.0   Principle of exchange

3.1   Be willing to provide the same type and level of information that you request from your benchmarking partner, provided that the principle of legality is observed.

3.2   Communicate fully and early in the relationship to clarify expectations, avoid misunderstanding, and establish mutual interest in the benchmarking exchange.

3.3   Be honest and complete.

## 4.0   Principle of confidentiality

4.1   Treat benchmarking **findings** as confidential to the individuals and organizations involved. Such information must not be communicated to third parties without the prior consent of the benchmarking partner who shared the information. When seeking prior consent, make sure that you specify clearly what information is to be shared, and with whom.

4.2   An organization's **participation** in a study is confidential and should not be communicated externally without their prior permission.

## 5.0   Principle of use

5.1   Use information obtained through benchmarking only for purposes stated to and agreed with the benchmarking partner.

5.2 The use or communication of a benchmarking partner's name with the data obtained or the practices observed requires the prior permission of that partner.

5.3 Contact lists or other contact information provided by benchmarking networks in any form may not be used for purposes other than benchmarking.

## 6.0 Principle of legality

6.1 If there is any potential question on the legality of an activity, you should take legal advice.

6.2 Avoid discussions or actions that could lead to or imply an interest in restraint of trade, market and/or customer allocation schemes, price fixing, bid rigging, bribery, or any other anti-competitive practices. Don't discuss your pricing policy with competitors.

6.3 Refrain from the acquisition of information by any means that could be interpreted as improper including the breach, or inducement of a breach, of any duty to maintain confidentiality.

6.4 Do not disclose or use any confidential information that may have been obtained through improper means, or that was disclosed by another in violation of a duty of confidentiality.

6.5 Do not, as a consultant, client or otherwise pass on benchmarking findings to another organization without first getting the permission of your benchmarking partner and without first ensuring that the data is appropriately 'blinded' and anonymous so that the participants' identities are protected.

## 7.0 Principle of completion

7.1 Follow through each commitment made to your benchmarking partner in a timely manner.

7.2 Endeavour to complete each benchmarking study to the satisfaction of all benchmarking partners as mutually agreed.

## 8.0 Principle of understanding and agreement

8.1 Understand how your benchmarking partner would like to be treated, and treat them in that way.

8.2 Agree how your partner expects you to use the information provided, and do not use it in any way that would break that agreement.

## ■ BENCHMARKING PROTOCOL

**BENCHMARKERS:**

➡ Know and abide by the European Benchmarking Code of Conduct.
➡ Have basic knowledge of benchmarking and follow a benchmarking process.
➡ Should have:
  ● determined what to benchmark
  ● identified key performance variables to study
  ● recognized superior performing organizations
  ● completed a rigorous internal analysis of the process to be benchmarked **before** initiating contact with potential benchmarking partners.
➡ Prepare a questionnaire and interview guide, and share these in advance if requested.
➡ Possess the authority to share and are willing to share information with benchmarking partners.
➡ Work through a specified contact and mutually agreed arrangements.

When the benchmarking process proceeds to a face-to-face site visit, the following behaviours are encouraged:

➡ Provide meeting agenda in advance.
➡ Be professional, honest, courteous and prompt.
➡ Introduce all attendees and explain why they are present.
➡ Adhere to the agenda.
➡ Use language that is universal, not one's own jargon.
➡ Be sure that neither party is sharing proprietary or confidential information unless prior approval has been obtained by both parties, from the proper authority.
➡ Share information about your own process, and, if asked, consider sharing study results.
➡ Offer to facilitate a future reciprocal visit.
➡ Conclude meetings and visits on schedule.
➡ Thank your benchmarking partner for sharing their process.

## BENCHMARKING WITH COMPETITORS

The following guidelines apply to both partners in **a** benchmarking encounter with competitors or potential competitors:

➡ In benchmarking with competitors, ensure compliance with competition law.

➡ Always take legal advice before benchmarking with competitors. Note: When cost is closely linked to price, sharing cost data can be considered to be the same as price sharing.)

➡ Do not ask competitors for sensitive data or cause the benchmarking partner to feel they must provide such data to keep the process going.

➡ Do not ask competitors for data outside the agreed scope of the study.

➡ Consider using an experienced and reputable third party to assemble the 'blind' competitive data.

➡ Any information obtained from a benchmarking partner should be treated as you would treat any internal, confidential communication. If 'confidential' or 'proprietary' material is to be exchanged, then a specific agreement should be executed to indicate the content of the material that needs to be protected, the duration of the period of protection, the conditions for permitting access to the material, and the specific handling requirements that are necessary for that material.

**Important Notice: This Code of Conduct is not a legal document. Though all due care has been taken in its preparation, the authors and sponsors will not be held responsible for any legal or other action resulting directly or indirectly from adherence to this Code of Conduct. It is for guidance only and does not imply protection or immunity from the law.**

# INDEX

# Becoming the Best

## How to Gain Company-Wide Commitment to Total Quality

### Revised Edition

Barry Popplewell and Alan Wildsmith

*A Gower Novel*

How could it happen in a buoyant market? New products, lots of orders, and yet no profit - a big fat ZERO. No doubt about it, the opportunity had been there, a chance to change the fortunes of the company. And he'd blown it. The stark reality of the year-end report was staring Neil Johnson in the face; the promised improvements in results just hadn't happened. The warning bells had been ringing long enough and the shareholders wouldn't continue to accept nil dividends. Something had to be done. *Becoming the Best* tells the story of how Neil Johnson turned his company round. But it took a cancelled order from his biggest customer to show him the way.

As the story unfolds, Neil begins to understand the problem. Quality is the key - not just product quality but total quality. 'If everybody was the *best* at what they do', he thought 'then this would be one hell of a company.' So that's what he sets out to do - become the best. How he conceives his idea, translates it into practice, cajoles and carries his employees with him is the story of this fascinating book.

This reissue comprises a copy of this bestselling business novel and a 32 page audit *Determining Business Excellence* to enable you to assess your own organization.

# Gower

# Best Practice Benchmarking

## Sylvia Codling

Benchmarking is potentially the most powerful weapon in the corporate armoury. It's the technique that enabled Cummins Engine Company to slash delivery time from eight months to eight weeks, Lucas to reduce the number of shopfloor grades at one of its sites from seventeen to four and British Rail to cut cleaning time for a 660-seat train to just eight minutes. In other companies order processing time has been brought down from weeks to days, engineering drawings output doubled and inventory cut by two-thirds.

And yet, in spite of the articles, the seminars and the conferences, managers continue to ask 'What is benchmarking?' and 'How do we do it?' The purpose of this book is to answer those questions. Through a series of case histories and references it shares the experience and knowledge acquired by benchmarking companies across a wide range of industries. Above all, it provides a detailed step-by-step guide to the entire process, including a complete set of planning worksheets.

Case studies include: Siemens Plessey, Volkswagen, British Rail, Lucas Industries, Shell, Rover and Hewlett Packard.

Benchmarking is a flexible discipline that has become a way of life in some of the world's most successful organizations. Learning from the best can help your own company to become a world leader in those areas that are

# Gower

# The Complete Guide to People Skills

Sue Bishop

As a manager wanting to get the most out of your team, you need to practise 'people-focused leadership'. You need to encourage your people to contribute fully to the success of your organization, and to do that, you need an armoury of people skills.

Sue Bishop's book provides a comprehensive guide to all of the interpersonal skills that you need to get the best from your team. Skills that you can apply in formal settings, such as recruitment interviews, or appraisals, as well as less formal, such as coaching or counselling. Team skills to help you communicate with, and develop, your people. Skills to handle disciplinary matters, or emotional crises, or to resolve conflict. And skills that you can use when you are just chatting with and enthusing individuals and the team.

*The Complete Guide to People Skills* is divided into two parts. Part I gives an overview of the core skills, and offers a brief explanation of some self-development and communication theories.

Part II shows how to apply these skills in different situations. It is arranged alphabetically by topic - from appraisals to teamwork. Each section includes an exercise to help you learn more about the skills and techniques and to apply them in your work.

# Gower

# Gower Handbook of Management Skills

## Third Edition

### Edited by Dorothy M Stewart

*'This is the book I wish I'd had in my desk drawer when I was first a manager. When you need the information, you'll find a chapter to help; no fancy models or useless theories. This is a practical book for real managers, aimed at helping you manage more effectively in the real world of business today. You'll find enough background information, but no overwhelming detail. This is material you can trust. It is tried and tested.'*

So writes Dorothy Stewart, describing in the Preface the unifying theme behind the Third Edition of this bestselling *Handbook*. This puts at your disposal the expertise of 25 specialists, each a recognized authority in their particular field. Together, this adds up to an impressive 'one stop library' for the manager determined to make a mark.

Chapters are organized within three parts: Managing Yourself, Managing Other People, and Managing the Business. Part I deals with personal skills and includes chapters on self-development and information technology. Part II covers people skills such as listening, influencing and communication. Part III looks at finance, project management, decision-making, negotiating and creativity. A total of 12 chapters are completely new, and the rest have been rigorously updated to fully reflect the rapidly changing world in which we work.

Each chapter focuses on detailed practical guidance, and ends with a checklist of key points and suggestions for further reading.

# Gower

# UK Product Development

## A Benchmarking Survey

Researched by Keith Nichols, Andy Pye and Colin Mynott

*A Design Council Report*

Over the last 30 years the UK has lost half its share of world manufactured exports. Companies are striving to improve performance and compete effectively in international markets, but are they doing enough? Is their performance really 'world class'?

Competitiveness no longer resides solely in manufacturing competency. Product development is now critical, and the development process is arguably the heartbeat of competitiveness. Yet despite these dramatic changes and the increasing availability of information, there are companies which still run with development processes established two or possibly three decades ago.

The *UK Product Development Survey* conducted by The Design Council set out to measure the performance of UK manufacturing companies and explore the key factors which determine product development ability. The survey was conducted among all the readers of *Engineering* magazine and the analysis brings together information received from over 500 companies spread across the whole range of industry in terms of size and sector. The results make enlightening (and sometimes alarming) reading, but above all demonstrate the need for companies to address the challenges now because there is evidence that very few of the best companies in this UK survey are in the same league as the best players in the world.

# Gower